The **Smart** Woman's Guide to Privacy Protection

An honest and practical look at privacy protection in both the physical and virtual world

By Alan Boulanger

www.smartwomansprivacy.com

ISBN-13: 978-0615631288
ISBN-10: 0615631282

This book is dedicated to my daughters and Stacy

Table of Contents

Preface:

"Wake up, Neo..."

Imagine someone you don't know looking through your purse or wallet and then entering your home to read your mail, rummage through your drawers, and read your diary. They wander outside and casually pick through your trash and find your empty prescription bottles and know you are prone to depression and are currently being treated for some personal ailment. They then attach a tracking device on you, bill you and now know where you are 24 hours a day/7 days a week. They know where you sleep...when you are at work... what you are thinking...

How would that make you feel?

How violated and angry would you feel?

This is what's happening every second, of every day – only you cannot see it.

Cyberspace today can be compared to the plot line of the popular movie, "The Matrix". In the Matrix, a sentient race of machines dominate a world where human beings are farmed and their energy is harvested for their sole benefit.

Humans trapped in the Matrix are fully immersed in a virtual reality construct; devised by the machines and designed to pacify the human population who are unaware of how they are being exploited.

In today's world, corporations such as Facebook, Google and LinkedIn, are the machines in the Matrix; however, instead of harvesting your bio-thermal energy, they are feeding off of your activities, both online and in the real world. They present you with services that you freely participate in and lull your suspicions with important sounding assurances like "Privacy Policies" and "Terms of Use Agreements". Have you ever really read any of the Terms of Use Agreements that you have consented to in the past?

If you are like most people, you cannot click that "Accept" button fast enough so you can get the half-price massage or play that game where funny cartoon birds are hurled against unsuspecting swine.

Sure, they have "Privacy Policies" in place, but they are, by and large, empty gestures. The only areas where a privacy policy violation could result in litigation are limited to children, financial/SSN, and medical related information.

So, what about your non-financial and non-medical information that is sitting both in your hand and on computers scattered throughout the world? What is protecting that information?

Nothing.

Background:

In the spring of 2012, I was reorganizing my house and I had wanted to get rid of several items, including a large old school tube television set. I didn't want to throw it away because it was still working and I would have to pay a fee at the dump. Plus, I didn't want to see something that was still functional sit in a landfill. I had tried advertising on Craigslist several times before, but I didn't even get a nibble. *Not that surprising as tube television sets are the modern day equivalent of the venerable fruitcake.* However, since the price was right on Craigslist (free), I thought I'd give it another go – and so, posted this ad:

Working 36" Stereo TV (Amherst)

Date: 2012-03-16, 1:14PM EDT
Reply to: *your anonymous craigslist address will appear here*

RCA with remote... $45,000.00 or free, either works for me

Within 20 minutes I had received my first email from a woman I will call "Jane". I replied that I would hold it for her and take down the ad. There is a delay between the time you request to take down a Craigslist ad and time the ad is actually removed from the systems. I then received a surprising number of queries for the beast to which I replied, "Sorry, it went quickly - at half-price". Offering steep discounts appears to be an effective way of getting rid of large bulky appliances.

Now back to Jane's email. She had expressed an interest in the television, ("free" worked better for her – can't win 'em all) and had requested that I write back to arrange for her to pick it up. It bothered me a little that a woman would respond using a personal email address to a complete stranger in cyberspace. At this point, I have her first name and an email address – *wasn't she aware of the risks of disclosing semi-private information to complete strangers?*

I mentally ran though a few scenarios worthy of B-grade horror movies and became a bit curious about what could be learned about our Ms. Jane, given the limited amount of information I had obtained from our initial contact.

Starting with her first name and an email address, I was looking at her front door via Google Street View in under 5 minutes.

Using a variety of free, publicly available resources, I was able to access her full name, phone number, date of birth, profession and photographs; I learned that she was recently divorced, who her ex-husband was, who her parents and grandparents were, that she was carrying a lot of debt and was behind on her bills, that she has children, suffered from fibromyalgia, where she worked, her work phone number, what kind of car she drove, and where she slept at night.

I then went though a few of the other responses from my Craigslist ad and did the same thing and was met with similar results.

I got a bad feeling in the pit of my stomach:

This is just wrong.

So why would I do this? What am I, some sort of hacker?

Kind of...

Back in the '90s, I had accepted a job building robots at a university and relocated my family to Amherst, MA, a vibrant little college town in Western Massachusetts. One day I noticed something odd on one of our computer systems and, long story short, we had become infected with hackers. Nice. I was able to fix our systems and, over the next few weeks, tracked the hackers around cyberspace all the way back to their secret clubhouse on a distant system. In the process, I discovered the home phone number of one of the hackers, the one with the handle "pmf".

I was annoyed that someone would have the nerve to break into one of my systems (and not give me a friendly heads up) and all I wanted was for these intruders to leave my systems alone. With the phone number in hand, I called the hacker known as, "pmf" at his home.

"A'llo?", with a noticeable British accent.

"Oh, Hi...Say, what are you doing in my systems at UMass?"

"Bloody Hell!!" <click>

I hung up the phone and burst out laughing. I had chased these little effing hacker punks through cyberspace and had just called one of them at his home. It was a well earned victory after several weeks of research, investigation and sneaky engineering. Just as my arm was tiring from patting myself on the back, my phone rang.

"This is Stacy Bauerschmidt of the U.S. Secret Service.....We need to talk."

And so began my unusual relationship with the Federal Government. I had inadvertently stumbled upon an active investigation by the U.S. Secret Service known as Operation CyberSnare – and the little punks I traced back to their lair – were actually professional hackers engaged in a profitable criminal enterprise.

My adventures of chasing hackers at UMass was brought to the attention of IBM Watson Research who was forming a new ethical hacking lab and they extended an invitation for me to join. I was glad to...and quickly learned that being a researcher at IBM without a PhD feels a little like being attractive enough to date, but not from a good enough family to bring home to meet the folks.

Nevertheless, I survived there for a number of years and since I was telecommuting, it freed me up to pursue my own technical interests and help out my new friends.

Over the next 12 years, I was an "off the books" asset and worked with the U.S. Secret Service, FBI, DEA, DOE, DOJ, U.S. Customs, along with an alphabet soup of Intelligence Agencies and consulted on security issues related to: Bank Fraud, National Security, Financial Institutional Extortion and Transnational Organized Crime Syndicates.

I've been invited to the NSA, CIA and the White House and found out first-hand that if you accidentally run a stop sign at CIA headquarters, people wearing shades and carrying automatic weapons get a little excited and that foreign agents cruising hotel bars can develop an accent after a few drinks.

In 1997, the FBI contacted me and asked me to provide technical assistance on the Citibank Russian Hacker case. In 1999, a federal prosecutor called on me for technical assistance on the Melissa Virus case.

I worked on a sexual-slavery case and located a young kidnapping victim at an oceanfront resort in Mexico (they got her out safe).

At times, I've donned a Kevlar vest and went along on pre-dawn raids on gangsters hideouts as part of the evidence collection team, *(once found a loaded, nickel plated, 9mm handgun between the couch cushions).* Members of the DEA consulted with me on providing secured communication channels for an operation and have developed technology and investigative techniques that are still in use today by law enforcement.

In the early 2000's I gave invited briefings to Secretary of the Treasury, Paul O'Neill and Richard Clark, of the United States National Security Counsel at 7 World Trade Center.

Immediately following the September 11th Terrorist Attacks, I was contacted and asked to provide technical assistance by the U.S. Secret Service and FBI.

During this active period, if a case involving hacking made the national media, there was an excellent chance I got a call.

I never asked for a dime and kept my mouth shut...

As someone with more than just a passing interest in Information Security, it concerns me that so much of our personal information is so casually strewn about the Internet. I had known that this type of information was out there – but this time it really bothered me.

It has simply become too easy.

Large corporations are making billions of dollars, feeding off of our activities and the real world consequences of this are not yet fully understood. Nearly everything you do - in both the real and virtual world - is recorded, stored, indexed, cross-referenced and data-mined. Facebook reported its ability to predict when you are about to experience a break up with your partner.

Can you imagine a time when these invasive systems start popping-up ads for couples counseling after you've just had a fight with your spouse? Or worse, start suggesting divorce lawyers and private investigators long before you're aware of any trouble in your relationship - all because they happen to have done some data-mining on your partner's online activities?

This systemic, automated invasion of our personal privacy is going on right now and it's completely invisible to us - and we allow it.

We collectively have to take some responsibility for our own actions. For years we have been happily sharing our personal information with people we do not know, for reasons we really do not fully understand.

Introduction:

This book is intended to help raise your awareness of the very serious issue of protecting your personal privacy in both the real and virtual world.

This is not about standing on the street corner shouting, *"We're all gonna die!"*, nor is it a "how-to" guide for angry creepers trying to make someone's life difficult. Its sole intention is to help raise your personal level of privacy awareness and give you the tools you need to take back control of your information that is floating around the Internet.

It is truly scary what is out there and this book can show you what you can do today to help protect your privacy, avoid annoyances, and most importantly, help protect your very person in the physical world. Contained within this book are easy to follow instructions that will show you how to locate your personal information and what you can do to get rid of it - from the source.

Although, if you are trying to hide from an Organized Crime Syndicate or the IRS, this book may not be addressing the level of privacy you would require: I would suggest speaking with a non-connected attorney first.

Stalking and Sexual Assault:

A friend of mine recently sent me this story:

> "I was on a dating site about 4 years ago. I was emailing (on the site) back and forth with this guy but he had no pic... he always seem to contact me at weird times of the day, but he explained it was because he was a "Cop" and he asked for my personal email address so he can send it to me so I gave it to him. And he sends me a pic and he is very attractive. So, now we talk on the cell phone and this goes on for some time, he is very concerned about me dating other people. I don't get it. So, I ask if he is married and he says, "No, no way." This goes on for awhile and then eventually he admits that he is separated. And I say, "I don't date separated guys. Get a divorce and call me." and he gets really upset. I hang up on him but he keeps calling back and texting. Real crazy stuff, like how in love he is with me and how I been playing him along and how he wants me and he is going to have me, blah, blah, blah... So, I just stop answering his calls and ignoring his texts. I am living in a house I own at this time and I am living with a friend of mine. I am watching a movie. Sitting in the living room with my dog. I get a call on my home phone which I don't answer, but I listen to the message.

> It's the “Cop”. He says, "I hope your enjoying your movie, I hate to spoil the ending, but eff it, I gonna anyways..." and he then tells me the ending of the movie. He then says, "You shouldn't have pissed me off. " (This man doesn't know my last name, I never gave out my home phone # and the blinds are drawn.) I have never been so scared in all my life."
>
> - Terri. Age 50

"But he seemed so nice."

It always starts off innocently.

A chance meeting at the grocery store. A posting on a social media website. The initial contact in an online dating service. Most of the time the interactions are pleasant and a new friend or lover is welcomed into our lives.

There are the other times when a new acquaintance, be it in the real world or in cyberspace, becomes a nuisance. For whatever the reason, when we decide to break off contact with this person, they get angry and vindictive and begin sending off nasty emails or leaving unpleasant voice mail messages.

In some cases, the situation can escalate into a harrowing ordeal that can result in a tragic, life altering event.

The trouble is, every single person we interact with, in both the physical and virtual world, has the potential of becoming our best friends and lovers but, this same person can become our stalkers and even our assailants.

Stalking Statistics:

- Every year more than 3.4 million people are victims of stalking. The average duration of stalking is nearly two years and even longer if the stalking involves intimate partners.

- One in twelve women (8%) and one in forty-five men (2%) will be stalked in their lifetimes. This figure only represents those cases that warranted police intervention. The true number of stalking victims is closer to one is six (16.6%) for woman and one in twenty-two (4.5%) men.

Source: http://bjs.ojp.usdoj.gov/content/pub/pdf/svus.pdf

The impact of stalking can be devastating and cause its victims to take drastic measures in their attempts to regain some control over their lives. These actions can range from changing their email address and cell phone number, to, in extreme circumstances, moving away and going into hiding.

Women are, by a wide margin, the most victimized by stalking. Not only do they have to be concerned about men stalking, but female-to-female stalking is estimated to account for 20% of all stalking incidents while male-to-male stalking has the fewest reports.

Stalkers come in all shapes and sizes and have different factors driving their behavior and many stalkers suffer from some form of mental illness.

I do not want to stigmatize those people who are burdened with a mental illness and address the fact that majority of people who suffer from a psychiatric disorder are not violent and are much more likely to become victims of violent crime than be the perpetrators. However, about 15-20% of those people suffering from a mental disorder, are prone to violence* and of that group, the illness can present as stalking behavior.

Source: Mullen's stalker typology (Psychiatry (Edgmont). 2008 August; 5(8): 37–42.):

The Rejected Stalker:

Stalks victim following end of relationship

The Intimacy Seeking Stalker:

Stalks seeking intimacy with victim; insists relationship exists

The Incompetent Stalker:

Lacks social skills; feels deserving of relation with victim.

The Resentful Stalker:

Stalking intended to frighten victim

The Predatory Stalker:

Stalking in preparation of physical or sexual attack.

One of the frustrating aspects of stalking for law enforcement is there is no single trait that can easily identify someone who is capable of stalking. Stalkers come in all shapes and sizes and from a variety of backgrounds.

Hodgins S, Mednick SA, Brennan PA, et.al. Mental disorder and crime. Archives of General Psychiatry 1996;53:489–496.

I have a former classmate I will call "Jeffrey", who was a smart and funny guy, but was not considered popular and viewed as being a little on the nerdy side. He would later be described as, "such a nice person" and "the kind of guy who walks grandmothers across the street".

Every year, "Jeffrey" would decide that some girl in our school was "The One" and he would then proceed to start giving her unwanted attention.

At first, he would just talk with her and they would joke back and forth. He would manage to see her frequently and then eventually the young woman would start dating some other guy and he would be crushed. The attention would then change from light and playful flirting to annoying pranks.

From what I knew, the pranks were harmless and I had never thought any of these actions were malicious in nature, just stupid kid stuff. The last time I saw "Jeffrey" was when I bumped into him in parking lot at the mall in Springfield, MA. We caught up and talked about our future and what our life plans were. He was extremely intelligent and was looking forward to a brilliant career in the technology or engineering fields.

On Valentine's day, in 1985, my girlfriend was watching television and a news report came on and she asked me if I knew a "Jeffrey Blah-blah". "Yes, why?"

"Jeffrey" apparently had resumed his habits from school but had advanced to the big leagues. He had selected another random woman from the college campus and she became "The One" in his mind. He showered her with unwanted attention and when he was ignored and rejected, he then began to harass her. When she spurned his advances on Valentine's day, he pulled out a pistol and emptied the weapon into her car - wounding her. The campus police, upon hearing the gunshots, tackled "Jeff" and seized his firearm. When they later searched his pickup truck, it was discovered he had brought along a "kit" consisting of ether, handcuffs and other assorted items. Killers often have similar "kits" - proof that every detail was thoroughly planned out.

"I had a **funny feeling** he's going to come after me," she later said at the trial.

"Jeffrey" was convicted and spent several years in the custody of the State. His victim was fortunate in some sense, and eventually recovered from her gunshot wounds. One of the bullets could not be removed and is a constant reminder of this event.

Several years pass by and in the early 90's "Jeffrey" is in the local news again. This time, he had selected the lead actress in his local community theater. At first, it was all innocent but as expected, things took a sinister turn and he began harassing her.

He sent her dead animals, coat hangers and notes referring to abortion. He looked up her alumni magazine and informed them that she had died of AIDS. This went on for a while until this young actress summoned up the courage and went to the police.

Upon receiving the report, the police went though "Jeffrey's" past behavior and decided to throw a net over him before the situation escalated further. The victim was smart in that she sought out help early.

"Jeffery" went away again for a probation violation, but his sentence was a gift to him; had the target of his affections done nothing and allowed the situation to escalate – "Jeffrey" could have murdered her and he would have been spending the rest of his life in prison. Instead, the police intervened and prevented a tragedy. "Jeffrey" was processed – served his time – and is currently married.

If you are being stalked, with or without your knowledge, you may never know what flavor of stalker has taken an interest in you.

It is best to raise your awareness and protect your privacy to help prevent a potential stalker from being able to cause you harm in the real world.

Sexual Assault Statistics:

- One in four college women report surviving rape (15 percent) or attempted rape (12 percent) since their fourteenth birthday.

- In a study by the U.S. Centers for Disease control of 5,000 college students at over 100 colleges, 20% of women answered "yes" to the question "In your lifetime have you been forced to submit to sexual intercourse against your will?" Thus, one in five college women has been raped at some point in her lifetime.

- In a typical academic year, 3% of college women report surviving rape or attempted rape. This does not include the summer, when many more rapes occur.

- There are 207,754 reports of sexual assault each year on people over the age of 12.

- Since only 54% of the incidents are reported, a realistic figure is 384,729 incidents per year.

The impact of a sexual assault is life altering. Considering 1 in 4 women will experience some form of sexual assault in their lifetime, it is very likely you are either a victim or are close to someone who has been assaulted and therefore have some insight of the long term, lingering, effects of this violent crime.

Physical vs.Virtual Worlds:

There have been instances where an exchange in the virtual world has lead to a tragedy in the physical world. This is why it's so important to be very careful of what information you are posting and to protect your personally identifiable information in the virtual world.

In September 2011, the murdered, mutilated, bodies of two young people were discovered hanging from a bridge in Mexico. Signs near the bodies claimed they were killed as punishment for their online posting denouncing the drug cartels.

One sign declared: "This is going to happen to all of those posting funny things on the Internet."

The other one sign read: "You better (expletive) pay attention. I'm about to get you."

The real question is, how did their attackers obtain this information? How did they pierce that membrane separating the virtual world from the physical world? But, on second thought, that question doesn't matter.

The problem is, once you disclose any information, you cannot "unpublish" it and have lost all control over its dissemination. This concept is so new, the act of attempting to remove information you have previously published, in other words "unpublish", is not even a word in the dictionary yet.

Results from Webster's Dictionary in 2012:

unpublish

"The word you've entered isn't in the dictionary. Click on a spelling suggestion below or try again using the search bar above."

The same is true whenever you send an email. Once it is sent, it's gone! There is no way to get it back or remotely delete the message, which is why it's so important that you be careful about what you send or post online.

The exponential growth of the Internet has fueled the exponential growth of the amount of your personal information that is being stored and shared with the rest of the world. For the first time in our history, information about anything and anyone, is available with just a few keystrokes and a mouse click.

Our human brains cannot fully grasp the magnitude of this rise of technology. We are not able to fully comprehend the consequences of having so much of our personal information at our fingertips and at the fingertips of others.

All of the large web service companies have privacy policies to calm our concerns - but they are just there to protect the corporation and not a promise to protect you. Only a few countries have effective privacy laws with any teeth. Most of the privacy policies in the United States have a clause stating they can change their privacy policy any time for any reason at their discretion and without your consent.

As an individual, you can get lured into disclosing your personal information, in part, because of the assurance of the website's privacy policies; but, without your consent any service can change the terms of their privacy policy and now our private information can be made available.

The privacy policy of Facebook stated that: *(on Mar 24, 2012)*

Notice of Changes

"If we make changes to this Privacy Policy we will notify you by publication here and on the Facebook Site Governance Page. If the changes are material, we will provide you additional, prominent notice as appropriate under the circumstances. You can make sure that you receive notice directly by liking the Facebook Site Governance Page."

So, what does this mean for you?

You probably have a lot of static individual personal information, (i.e., your name, location, email address, phone number, etc.,) as well as information about your activities, ("I've been accepted to Harvard!" or "Three days until my court date, I'm so nervous!!") and that data is sitting on the systems controlled by Facebook.

If any website decides to start sharing more of your personally identifiable information; either the static data you entered when registering your account, or your posted online activities – they can.

You are given some "assurances" but, since there is no financial or medical information involved, getting the authorities excited about divulging your personal data will be difficult. Facebook and other companies can make changes to the privacy policy and all they have to do is to provide you with some form of notification – all the while remaining in possession of your information.

Say, for example, a company decides to change their privacy profile and follows through with all of the legal requirements and complies with various laws, posting a notice that they intend to share more of your information than you are comfortable with. If you don't use this service frequently, you might not receive the notice, or the e-mailed copy was eaten up by your spam filter. It doesn't matter, your information is now at risk and there was nothing you can do about it.

That is the problem with "Privacy Policies", they are policies, like "Funny Hat Fridays" and are not contractual obligations to protect your information.

Corporations can and will change their privacy and data handling policies while they have control of your private information and these changes will be for their sole benefit and not yours. They will post their notifications of the change and it will be all nice and legal. There are laws protecting your identity, right?

Not really.

In the United States, the only information about adults that is protected under the various privacy laws is information related to children, financial account information, social security numbers, and medical records.

Everything else is fair game. So, any of the social media sites that have your personal information can change their policies and allow your image, name, address and postings to be inadvertently brought to the attention of various groups, like drug cartels, who apparently frown on postings critical of their organization.

Companies like Google, Facebook, Twitter, and LinkedIn, are in control of a large amount of your personal information and do take active steps to protect against gross violations of your privacy. However, their systems are not perfect. The computer systems running these services are massively complex machines running hundreds of millions of lines of code.

There will always be defects and mistakes that could put your privacy at risk in spite for their best intentions. It's a fact so the best bet is to be very aware of what information you are putting out there in the first place.

To paraphrase a line from the movie, "The Terminator": The Internet is out there! It can't be bargained with. It can't be reasoned with. It doesn't feel pity, or remorse, or fear. And it absolutely will not stop, ever..."

What is Personal Privacy?:

Personal Privacy related information is that information in cyberspace than can uniquely identify you in the physical world. All of our daily activities and various services we use are constantly leaking information that is recorded and preserved somewhere out there in cyberspace. Every piece of information tied to your identity or activity is a thread that can be pulled and potentially reveal more about you than you are comfortable revealing.

This electronic information can also contain hidden information, or meta-data, that is invisible and can be used to reveal information about you that you would consider private. For example, photos taken from a camera phone can be geotagged. That is the default setting. When a piece of data is geotagged, be in a photo, video or Facebook posts, the location of where the photograph is recorded and preserved.

If someone were so inclined to take a photo of themselves to send to a current or potential paramour, that exact location of where that photo was taken can be embedded in the image. If the person who receives the photo wishes to share that data – they can easily forward it to an email address or to another phone. In fact, any device receiving that image, can store and forward that photograph or video. Whenever the photo has been transmitted to another recipient, that location information is preserved. Any person or system with access to that photo will have the location of where that photo has been taken and will easily have enough information to generate driving directions to that exact spot.

There have been several instances of where a jilted lover posted a "Rape fantasy" on Craigslist and women have been attacked as a result. With geotagged intimate photos or videos, someone would only have to receive the photo to be able to extract the address of the subject as well as driving directions to their residence.

When people think about personal privacy, they tend to think about someone going through their mail, reading their diary or peeking though the window. This is true, but, too narrow a scope of what exactly privacy is about.

> **Privacy** (from Latin: *privatus* "separated from the rest, deprived of something, esp. office, participation in the government", from *privo* "to deprive"") is the choice that an individual can make to separate, and therefore isolate, themselves and, their related information, and then consciously choose how much of themselves is to be revealed to others.

In the physical world, we can make a conscious effort to protect our privacy. We can lock our doors, close the shades, hide our diaries, get an unlisted phone number and choose not to disclose our information to people we do not know.

In the virtual world, we really have no idea of what is happening with our information. The privacy policies are supposed to inform us about what information is being collected and how our information is being handled, but there is no way to verify that these policies are actually being followed.

Our privacy is one of those things that is easily ignored until it is violated and has an impact on us in the real world. It touches every area of our lives: from where we live, where we get our education, to who we love, how much money we make...and everything in between; this information is very valuable to corporations.

Value of Personal Information:

Corporations do not want to be spending their advertising dollars sending BMW brochures to people living in tin-roofed cabins in the backwoods.

They want to make sure that their advertising budget is efficiently spent and will reap a measurable return on investment. This is not evil, in and of itself, however, it does make perfect sense. If you are a CEO of a large corporation, you would not want to squander your advertising budget on ineffective marketing and so have a strong motivation to ensure that your products are only advertised to those consumers that fit the profile of your target market.

This is the genius behind Google.

If you are searching for a particular consumer product, there is a pretty good chance that you will want to purchase this product – else why bother looking for it? Combine that with best-of-breed search technology, and you have a company that can afford to offer perks like, Boeing 767s to their top executives.

There is a huge profit motive for the collection and storage of your personal activities, in both the real and virtual world. Data on all of your activities is collected, stored, analyzed and data-mined to generate a consumer profile commodity that can be sold to interested companies. This is why corporations want to track your activities across the Internet.

This is why Facebook, a massive threat to Google, wants you to use their login service everywhere. Facebook collects your personal information, that you volunteer, and your activities, that you may have unknowingly volunteered.

Sure it's convenient, but why would Facebook offer this free service? To track your activities on other services as well. The reason Facebook is a threat to Google is Facebook can offer corporations a more detailed, intimate, consumer profile than Google.

Google knows what you are searching for.

Facebook knows when you stepped in dog-doo.

This level of intimacy is sought by all the advertising networks - but it can backfire. If a young mother is searching or talking about baby related items online, Google, Facebook and other online marketing corporations, know this person is interested in products and services that will help her raise her child. However, if she then suffers a miscarriage, the distraught mother will spend the next year viewing ads for child related products.

If you are a mother who has suffered a loss and do not want to receive child-related marketing material– contact your vendors ASAP and remove your name from their mailing lists. Clear your search history on Google and other search engines and remove any references on Facebook or other social media sites.

This is what we are up against and so we need to be very aware of the information that we are giving away, and be even more aware of the information that is being taken without our knowledge.

As mentioned earlier, all it took was an email address and a little curiosity and I had more information about an individual that they would be uncomfortable with disclosing to me face-to-face.

Each chapter of this book will outline the things that you can do today to help ensure your privacy in the future. Since one size does not fit all, each of the privacy enhancement sections will offer options so you can select what level of privacy, and risk tolerance, you are most comfortable with.

Levels of Privacy Awareness:

You can think of levels of privacy awareness in these terms:

Jane Q' Public:

This is the default level of privacy. By default level, I'm referring to anyone accepting the default levels of assurances that are provided by the services they use. They have done little to nothing to modify the default privacy levels of their virtual and physical worlds.

Risk tolerance of this group can primarily be attributed to ignorance of the potential impact on their life. If they had known, they would likely want to advance to the next level.

Secret Agent:

After someone has a few annoying experiences, this group may have unintentionally graduated to the Secret Agent level of privacy awareness. They might have taken some basic precautions, such as, unlisted phone number and adjusting their privacy setting on Facebook and other social media sites to help minimize the amount of unwanted attention.

This is often not enough and so, these people have developed an increased sense of privacy awareness and likely have a managed privacy practice employed in both the virtual and physical world.

Witness Protection:

This is the most extreme level of privacy awareness; almost to the point of paranoia. Some people might confuse this level of privacy anxiety with people suffering from mental illness, but this level applies to people who are in hiding because of a catastrophic life altering event – such as stalking or sexual assault. Anyone at this elevated level will possess a very low-risk tolerance, are very aware of their personal privacy, and have most likely employed a comprehensive privacy protection plan.

Once you select the level of privacy you wish to maintain, you will have to be conscious of the many subtle ways that your information can be disclosed without your knowledge and take the necessary precautions to protect yourself. A person who is very concerned about protecting their privacy may have to reconsider opening up a Facebook account and posting their private information. A person who is in the Secret Agent level of awareness, may want to exercise caution when sending their physical location to people they do not know.

The level of privacy you select is your personal choice and you will have to be vigilant in ensuring that it is being maintained and not inadvertently violated by your actions or the actions of others.

Financial Identity Theft:

This book is not focused on protecting yourself against identity theft; it's about helping to protect your privacy in the real world and financial identity theft can have a significant negative impact on you in your life. By employing the recommendations throughout this book, you can help better protect your financial identity and reduce the chances that you will become a victim. There are several simple things you can do right now to help protect your financial identity.

Step 1:

If you haven't already, get a copy of your free credit report as soon as possible. Don't fall for the ads on television with the hipster and the catchy song. Go to the only authorized source of free annual credit reports allowed by law:

www.AnnualCreditReport.com

A link to this site is available on the Federal Trade Commission's website (www.ftc.gov) under the Free Credit Reports tab.

After you have received your copy, go though the report and make sure you recognize all of your active and inactive accounts. If you find anything you are not aware of, file a dispute with the credit reporting agency. Remember to also look at who is pulling your credit reports – *I had brought my car in for service last year and later learned that someone had pulled my credit report. Needless to say, we had a nice chat on the phone and I received a free oil change – at least I hope I did.*

If there are any accounts that you are not currently using, consider closing them down. It may not be worth the headache of having too many open accounts.

Step 2:

Get yourself two credit cards, from two different financial institutions and try to get rid of the rest. If you carry other credit cards, try to minimize the number of the credit cards you have.

If you feel you must maintain more than two credit cards, then you can rotate your cards and use only two at a time.

Many of the credit card vendors offer virtual credit card numbers that act as an alias and can be used online. These come in "single use", and "use anywhere" flavors. With the single use card, if you want to shop with another online vendor, you would have to generate another virtual card number and enter that information into the payment information section whereas the "use anywhere" cards act as a regular credit card number. Whether you use two separate accounts or many virtual accounts is a personal choice.

Step 3:

Limit both credit cards to a credit limit that is equal to 1.5-2.0 times your monthly credit card purchases in the last year. The credit card companies will want to give you a higher credit limit. Call them and request they reduce the credit limit to the minimum that you would need.

This is to help minimize your "worst case scenario" in the event that your account is compromised and the credit card company, for whatever the reason, refuses to reimburse you and hold you accountable for the unauthorized charges.

If you ever need to increase your credit card spending limit, the issuing companies will be more than happy to help you out. As soon as you no longer need the increased limit, call the issuer and reduce your liability by reducing your credit spending limit.

Step 4:

One credit card is to be used only in the real world (i.e.,Target, Wholefoods, Victoria's Secret, etc.).

This is your "**Clean**" credit card – *you know where it's been.*

Your other card is only to be used to make purchases online (i.e., iTunes, Amazon, eBay, etc.)

This is your "**Dirty**" credit card – *you don't know where it's been.*

By separating your virtual financial activities from your real world financial activities, you are better able to monitor your accounts for unusual activity and unauthorized use. If your account is ever compromised, it will be easier to track down the source of the breach.

Watch for transactions that are small, under five dollars, from sources you do not recognize. These could be signs that your credit card has been sold on the black market and these small debit/credit events are part of the underground verification process. If you see any of these activities on your statement – alert your credit card company immediately.

If you are very concerned about your online business activities, there is a simple solution. Gift Cards and pre-paid Visa cards! Go to your local store and you can purchase gift cards that you can use to make purchases online. The beauty of this is you can also pay in cash. After you purchase a gift card, be sure to call the 1-800 number on the back and verify the redemption value. Scammers in the past have copied the gift card ID and then wait a few days to call the 1-800 number to get the balance. Once they learn that the card has been activated, they will use the copied ID to make purchases. Only buy gift cards that have a protected PIN on the back and be aware of any signs of tampering.

Step 5:

Another way to better protect your personal finances is to never, ever, ever, use your debit/ATM cards to make any purchases in any way, at any time, ever. The reason for this is the laws governing debit/ATM cards are different from the laws regulating credit cards.

If your debit card gets compromised, then all of the money in your personal account can disappear in an instant and it could take months to get your money back; plus, you can be still held accountable for the entire amount! That's a long to time to have zero balance and is simply not worth the risk for a little convenience.

Always use a credit card - without exception.

Step 6:

Your debit/ATM card should only be used at ATMs owned by your bank. If you cannot find your bank's ATM then "Plan B" would be to use an ATM from another large bank. Under no circumstance, unless it's a dire emergency, use the privately owned, free-standing ATMs you see in the mall, bars, or at gas stations. These ATMs are not to be trusted.

Criminals in the past have put up ATMs for the sole purpose of collecting debit card credentials. *This happened to a friend of mine at the time of this writing – she used the ATM at a gas station and within a day there were unauthorized charges on her account.*

Step 7:

Spend a few bucks and get a good cross-cut shredder and use it early and often. Meth-heads, or people addicted to methamphetamine, have a lot of time, and even more energy, at their disposal to go to the dump off hours and rummage though the garbage looking for something they can use to commit identity theft.

Once they have enough of your trash, they can piece together poorly shredded documents and obtain access to your accounts and go merrily on their way to the local Walmart to try to buy a pallet of Sudafed and lithium batteries. *They won't be able to, as Walmart and other retailers have controls in place.*

Step 8:

Contact your bank and submit a request to "opt-out" of sharing any of your private information outside of the bank. This will help prevent your bank, entrusted with your most sensitive details, from sharing anything to third-parties. One of the unintended consequences is that you'll likely get less junk-mail, so you might have to find another way to heat your home.

Step 9:

If you use an online payment service like PayPal, open up a separate bank account with about $100 in it. Then go to the service provider, in this case Paypal, and use that account number along with your dirty credit card number. This is to provide a safety barrier between your personal finances and online payment service providers. If there is a security breach, losing $100 is much better than losing your entire checking account.

If you ever suspect you are a victim of financial identity theft, act promptly. The first place to visit for more information on what you need to do is the Federal Trade Commission's website:

www.ftc.gov/idtheft

These simple steps can help you better protect your financial information and help reduce the risk that you will become a victim of identity theft. Now that your financial information is a bit more manageable we can now address the other privacy issues that can impact your life in the real world.

Smartphone Privacy:

If you and your smartphone were able hop into a time machine and transport yourself back to the early 1990's - a mere 20 years ago - and told people that you had been abducted by aliens but had escaped and snatched this weird device from their spaceship – they wouldn't think you were crazy until after they saw you buying a ton of Apple stock.*

By any measurement the smartphone is a technological wonder. It can - well you know what your smart phone does - but what you might not know is that your favorite personal device could be betraying you as you read this.

If your old cellphone is turned on and registered to a cell tower in the carrier's network, the physical location of that cellular tower is known by the carrier.

**Note to nerds: The smartphone would not work on the old AMPS cellular phone network used in the late 80's early 90s' networks and Wi-Fi/Internet, while invented, was not widely deployed – however, the basic non-Internet capabilities should be sufficiently impressive to support the alien abduction claim.*

The registration code your cellphone used to authenticate itself to the tower is known by the carrier; the strength of the radio signal used to carry out this authentication process can be measured by applying a few formulas. The carrier can now estimate your distance to the cellphone tower. When they employ the relative strengths of several cellular towers, the carrier would have enough information to be able to triangulate these signals and get the location of your handset to within several meters.

The older smartphones used this method to obtain the location information for use in the integrated mapping application. The new smartphones use the Global Positioning Satellite (GPS) system to identify your location. By using these techniques – the smartphone is capable of determining your location to within feet. Personally, I find it a bit unsettling that I can track my location from my bed to my bathroom in my own home.

When you purchased your smartphone, the first piece of personally sensitive information is the phone number supplied by your carrier. This sequence of numbers is your unique identity in the electronic world and a direct link to you in the physical world.

When you received your smartphone, you performed the initial set up, then set up your email accounts; now you have a name, an email address and your phone number. Your cellphone carrier has that information as well, along with where you live and your bank or credit card information depending on how you pay your cell phone bill.

What makes smartphones so powerful is their ability to run mobile applications. After your smartphone is provisioned with your basic account information and configured, you can then take your new electronic friend home and start downloading mobile applications.

Those mobile applications, or apps, that you have loaded onto your cell phone may have access to the private information stored on your device. When installing the mobile app, you will be prompted to grant permission to allow the app to access your personal data and some of the underlying features of your device.

Most people are unaware of the implications of granting an app access to your personal information. The problem is that by granting access to your information, you are not fully informed about what that app is doing with your information. While you allowed access to your personal information, you may not have realized that the app could send your personal information, along with your physical location to remote systems while you play some mind numbing game. These apps request access to your private information, but the apps do not to tell you what they will do with this information once you have granted them permission. Even if they do tell you, you have no way of knowing what the app is really doing with your data.

Like a Victorian Era pickpocket, your smartphone's new mobile app is distracting you with flashing lights and funny sounds while, quite possibly, accessing and transmitting your personal data to some remote system without your knowledge or consent.

In March 2012, a class action lawsuit was filed by the Austin, Texas law firms of Edwards Law, Carl F. Schwenker and the Jordan Law Firm against 18 companies: Path, Twitter, Apple, Facebook, Beluga, Yelp!, Burbn, Instagram, Foursquare, Gowalla, Foodspotting, Hipster, LinkedIn, Rovio, ZeptoLab, Chillingo, Electronic Arts and Kik Interactive. The complaint of the lawsuit is the "surreptitious" gathering of information about users of mobile apps made by these companies.

One of the more disturbing capabilities of the smartphone is its ability to track you and report your exact position in real time. Think about it. If a phone is on your person as you go about your daily activities and some mobile app is secretly recording your location and sending your position to a remote system without your knowledge, then someone, or something, out there knows where you are at all times, as well as know where you *are not*.

Say you post a status update on your Facebook page with a photo of a martini and a status update that says:

"Finally! What a long day!!".

It is possible that your photo has been geotagged with your exact position on this planet by your smartphone and now Facebook knows where you are within a few meters.

The Facebook smartphone app, if in the default configuration, will geo-tag your status update with your rough location - such as the town in which your are enjoying your well deserved martini.

The simple act of updating your status has just reported your physical location to all of your "friends", and possibly "friends-of-friends" and perhaps even complete strangers. The picture of the martini could also contain enough detail in the background or on the napkin with the bar's name. Now all these people know exactly where you are.

This may not be a problem in and of itself. The problem is that it also reveals where you currently are not. With simple calculations anyone will know how long it will take you to get from where you are now, to where you will be and potentially, how much time they have.

Burglar/Crackhead:

How much time to enter and rob your house – especially, if you're far away on vacation

Naughty Child:

How much time to hide the alcohol and get the funny smell out of the house.

Jealous Partner:

How much time to read your diary/emails and install a key-logger on your laptop

Personal Stalker:

Where to get a drink to watch you.. and watch you... and watch...

Fr-enemy:

Just adding to the list to cause trouble later.

Cheating Partner:

How much time they have left to "entertain" their guest(s)

Creepy Roommate:

How much time to go rummaging though your dirty laundry.

Another risk arises when someone attempts to be deceptive. Say a someone bumps into an old love interest and wants to meet her or him for coffee, but told their current partner that they are out with the guys at "The Spoke".

That bar is in Amherst but this person was really at a cafe in Springfield getting themselves reacquainted.

If they tried to be slick and post a picture (taken earlier) and update, or tweet, their status "Good to see the guys!!" on their smartphone, Facebook/Twitter accounts, these services could out them by tagging the post as originating from "near Springfield" instead of Amherst and they might have some 'splaining to do when they get home later that evening.

Granted these are extreme examples, but they are to illustrate a point and that point is there can be unintended consequences of disclosing your physical location to people you may or may not know. So, to be safe, try to keep your personal location private.

Safe Sexting:

People send "sexy" pictures from their smartphones. It happens. Don't judge. The problem with taking any questionable pictures on a mobile device is that you cannot guarantee that you will retain control of your device in the future.

There have been many incidents where people have their cellphone or laptop/tablets, lost or stolen and the sensitive information these devices held were disclosed and embarrassed its owner. Similar risks are incurred when taking a photograph that you would be uncomfortable wearing on a t-shirt out in public, and then sending that image to another system, be it cellphone, or email address. You have since lost control of that image.

It's gone.

You cannot rely on the assurances of the recipient that they will delete them, *"Oh, hi baby - yeah, I deleted 'em..heh heh"*, but they can just as easily store and forward the images to other devices.

One of the many problems with this is you cannot guarantee that the receiver will be able to maintain control over their own device. If their mobile device is lost or stolen, anyone with possession of that device now has, not only a compromising image of you, but also a direct link to you in the real world.

If your smartphone is in the 'default' mode, then that image you have just sent contains hidden information, the GPS coordinates, of the physical location of where that photo was taken. That information, is encoded in the meta-data of that image and, unless stripped out, will follow that image until every last copy has been deleted or destroyed.

If you or someone you know got a little tipsy and sent a few enticing photos to a potential paramour, you need to remember that every system, including the people who maintain those systems between you and the receiver has a copy of this image, as well as the directions to your home.

If you're using one of the “storage in the cloud” backup services, like iCloud, then your photo was automatically uploaded onto the storage server and is now accessible to every device registered to that account as well as the people who are maintaining each of those systems. This is the best case scenario! A possible worst case scenario would be to drunk-text the image to a wrong number whose owner just happens to have escaped from prison and has a penchant for Japanese hack-n-slash horror porn and now has directions to your home. Sounds like the plot line to B-movie, but, it is technically possible.

Be aware that there are porno websites out there such as, www . isanyoneup . com, that encourage people to upload their n00die pix and links to their Facebook profile. There is nothing preventing your new friend from submitting your photos to these websites, or emailing them to their friends who can then submit them without your permission. *(If you want to visit this site or similar adult sites, do so from your home computer and not from a work computer or in a coffee shop.)*

As with safe sex in the real world, the only way to be 100% safe is to not do it at all. However, if you want to sext, do so safely and not have your location or any uniquely identifiable information in your love notes – like your face or your tattoo.

At first, these nifty gizmos were a welcome convenience and now, these intrusive devices have been transformed into a dangerous and disloyal distraction. So, before we rise up and collectively smash our beloved gadgets in front of fan boys milling about outside the Apple Store, let's take a step back, and remember two basic truths:

1 - We ***OWN*** these devices.

2 - They are here to serve ***US****!*

One quick, simple, way to begin this process is to ask yourself one question:

"If I knew I would lose my phone tomorrow to my worst enemy, what would I do today?"

Securing your Smartphone:

The following chapter is to help you secure your smartphone to a "reasonable" level of security and privacy. I say reasonable because you can never be 100% sure that your device is playing by the rules. However, you can improve the privacy of your mobile device by doing a few simple things right now. If you have Witness Protection level of privacy concerns, then you probably should not own a smartphone at all. If you decide that you must have a cellphone, then go to Walmart and pay cash for a pay-as-you-go phone.

If you are in the super-duper ultra-top secret level of privacy awareness, then go buy a case of "pay-as-you-go" phones and only use them once before wiping them clean and tossing them out the window as you pass over a bridge.

For the rest of us, we can do a few simple things to better protect our mobile privacy.

Physical Security:

It's very important that you maintain the physical security of your mobile device. Never leave it unattended.

Not on the bar, in your car, on the table, or when you use the restroom. Always have it on your person and not hanging out of your back pocket. Anyone with physical access to your cellphone will likely be able to access its contents in spite of your security precautions. If you always maintain the physical security of your cellphone, you will have much less to worry about in the future.

Screen Lock:

The screen lock is used to help prevent people who have physical control of your mobile device from accessing its contents. Always employ the screen lock feature of your device and set it to a time setting you are comfortable with.

Select a pass-code that is easy for you to remember, but cannot be tied to you. Do not use your phone number, birthday or the last 4 digits of your Social Security Number. When entering your code, try to avoid allowing anyone to witness you entering your code. Some people have a special talent that can guess your pass-code simply by watching you as you enter it.

The screen lock feature is, unfortunately, not foolproof. In the past the screen lock on both the iPhones and Android phones could be bypassed for nearly every version of the operating system available. For proof, enter "screen lock bypass" in your favorite search engine and see the results.

The screen lock on your cellphone is a lot like a bicycle lock. It'll keep people from casually walking away with your bike, but if someone really wants it, they have the tools and techniques to be able to bypass the security device and steal your ride.

CallerID:

CallerID is that setting that will allow you to block your phone number from being disclosed to the person you have called. When making calls to people or numbers you do not know, have your CallerID turned off. If someone asks to borrow your phone to make an emergency call, turn off CallerID before you hand your phone over.

Remember, this sequence of numbers is a *direct link to you in the real world,* so protect it - only give it out to people and organizations you really trust.

We all know that CallerID can help protect your phone number when making phone calls. However, disabling CallerID can lull you into a false sense of security. Regardless of your CallerID settings, anytime you send a text message from your cellphone, your phone number is displayed on the receiving handset. Try this yourself:

> Shut off your CallerID and try calling your friend sitting next to you - *your number is blocked.*
>
> Next, send them a text - *now your number is displayed.* What? Didn't you just tell your phone to protect your phone number?

There is currently no way to disable this* so, try to avoid sending a text message to someone you do not know if you want to protect your cellphone number.

Blocking your CallerID can help, but it does not provide 100% protection for your phone number. Anytime you call a 1-800 or 1-900 number your phone number will be displayed and calls to any regular phone number can be bounced to a 1-800 number and cause your phone number to be disclosed to the person, or organization that had subscribed to the 1-800 service. While blocking CallerID is not perfect, it does offer enough protection for the average person.

Location Services:

Location services is your smartphone's ability to "know" your exact location in the real world and report that location to the service provider and your mobile applications.

During the activation process you were prompted to enable this service and it is very likely that is the current setting. My personal cellphone has this feature disabled until I need it.

You can opt to shut this service off completely if you are concerned about your location privacy. However, this feature will be enabled without your knowledge in the event of emergencies and the location information will be provided to emergency responders. You don't have a choice, but that's not a bad thing.

** I have recently filed a fix for this issue.*

If you choose to enable the location services, you can rein them in by configuring your smartphone to limit access to your location information to those applications that you think are entitled to it.

The mapping application has a legitimate use of your current position. This service is helpful and will help you get to where you need to go. As long as you are aware and comfortable with the possibility that this information is being sent to your service provider or manufacturer, then enabling this service should not be a problem.

On the other hand, your camera does not need access to your GPS coordinates. This is dangerous because by enabling this feature, every photo and even video, could be tagged with the exact position of where that image was taken.

If you took a photograph that you might be embarrassed about when you sobered up, the location of that compromising position is recorded for posterity and will follow that image for as long as the image exists on your handset and even on all of the automatic backup services. It's probably best to have this feature disabled on your phone.

You took the picture – you should have no problem remembering where it was taken.

Social media applications do not need access to your exact position. Facebook, LinkedIn, Twitter et al, can be denied access to your location. If this feature was allowed, then every post you make or every photo you take could be tagged with your exact location and posted for the world to see.

As we've seen, posting your location also tells the world where you are not – and how long it will take you to get to where you will be in the future. Ask yourself how this helps you?

Other Mobile Applications:

You can go through your entire list of applications and decide if you want these applications to have access to your physical location. Again, some have a legitimate reason for this access (i.e., maps, weather, etc.) but be very careful which mobile apps you allow access to your location information. A fun game really doesn't really need to know where you are for you to play it.

Wi-Fi/Bluetooth:

Wi-Fi and Bluetooth services are used to communicate with the Internet and to other wireless devices. These features can be turned off until they are needed. They can always be turned on later for the period in which they are used, then immediately turned off.

There are several reasons for this level of privacy. Both the Wi-Fi and Bluetooth features contain unique information that can identify your mobile device and therefore can potentially track you.

There are rogue Wi-Fi/Bluetooth access points in public places, like airports, that will try to automatically connect to your device. When a rogue access point connects to your device, it can attempt to monitor all of the information to and from your smartphone.

If you have a mobile application running that contains your credentials, a rogue access point can try to steal these credentials when the app attempts to phone home or access the back-end services.

Many mobile apps are well written and do provide some level of "session security" - but not all do, so it's risky to have your wireless data service on at all times.

Location Based Mobile Apps:

Location based mobile applications are services that use your physical location and allow you to "check-in" to restaurants and other social locations.

As we've seen, there are risks associated with broadcasting your physical location and time information to systems and people you may or may not know.

In 2012, there was a mobile app called "Girls Around Me" that used the location services on mobile phones. The app used this feature as well as information from social media service providers to create a radar-like image of where women were located. Anonymously – these women did not know someone was tracking them. When the media published an article about this mobile app, it was pulled from the app-store over the public outcry.

Using location based apps is a personal preference. I am privacy aware and personally, don't really need to know where all of my peeps are at and feel it would be a bit narcissistic of me to assume that they would care where I am. Sending a text is easier and safer. But, again, it is your choice.

Voice Mail:

With your new found sense of privacy awareness, call yourself on your cellphone and listen to the outgoing message. The default for many carriers is to have an adenoidal female computer-generated voice stating the number you have dialed. This is perfect. The intelligence community uses this technique as it's an effective way to convey a message without disclosing any additional information by only repeating the information the caller already knows. If it's good enough for James Bond, it'll probably work for you.

If you have recorded a personal outgoing voice mail message, be careful not to disclose your name or other uniquely identifiable information. If you must have a personalized outgoing message – you can repeat the script from the automated default setting and simply state: "You have dialed 555-2525, please leave a message at the tone – thank you" or "Hi! Leave a message!". The only thing you have additionally revealed is the sound of your voice, your approximate age, and your gender. This is why the default, automated, setting provides the best privacy.

Contact List:

Consider using first names only, or better yet, initials, in your contact list to better protect the privacy of your family and friends on your mobile device. This is because if you lose control of your mobile device, anyone with it can use your contact list to either contact you or annoy and harass your family, friends and business contacts.

Application Security:

Be very careful about what mobile applications you allow to reside on your mobile device. Assume that every application is potentially dangerous and will attempt to collect information about you for the publisher's benefit. Recall that lawsuit filed in Austin this year where applications were collecting personal information without the user's knowledge.

If the mobile application prompts you to grant access to any service the application should not need – then deny the request and delete the application.

If you want to play a game, but are not sure if you trust the application, then you can always elect to install the game and then delete it when you are done playing. This will help prevent the app from running in the background and possibly spying on you.

Unless you have access to the source code of the app, as well as the source code for your mobile device, you cannot be 100% sure of what your app is doing with your information and with your device.

If the mobile application requires credentials, make sure to configure the application so it does not keep you logged in if the application is related to financial or personally identifiable information.

The mobile apps for Facebook, LinkedIn, Twitter, your Bank, Amazon, eBay and others can be logged out when you are done using them. It is very convenient to keep yourself logged in, but if you lose control of your mobile device, and there's a good chance you will, think about what could happen with unauthorized access to these services. If you log in every time you use the mobile app, it will help you remember all of your user names and passwords.

Email Accounts:

If you are like many people, you probably have several email accounts provisioned on your mobile device. Go through each of these accounts and send an email to one of your other email accounts.

Then, go onto a computer, like your laptop that you may have already secured, and look at these emails. Is there any identifiable information contained in the emails that you are uncomfortable with disclosing to potential recipients? If so, then go into the email account settings section of your smartphone and adjust the settings accordingly and remove the information you wish to remain private.

As a general rule, for real accounts, your first name will suffice. For your garbage accounts, either blanks or just a few random initials will be sufficient.

Under your Mail, Contact and Calendar settings, go through each of the accounts and make sure that something called "TLS" and/or "SSL" is enabled on both the sending and receiving of email. This is because if TLS/SSL security was not enabled then any device from your smartphone to the email server you are connecting to could have access to your login credentials and therefore have access to your accounts. Like many people, if you share those credentials with other services, then they will also have access to those other services as well.

Call History / Texts / Browser History:

Consider turning off text message preview. If someone sends you a text message while the phone is sitting on the counter, then everyone in the immediate area will be able to view the contents of the message. Only view text messages after you enter in the screen lock code - out of view.

Text messages and your call history should be purged frequently. There's no reason to keep this information on your mobile device. By periodically paring down and removing any information that is not necessary, you greatly reduce the impact in the event your cellphone is lost or stolen.

For web browsing on your mobile device, tighten up the security and privacy settings. This will help prevent your mobile Internet browsing activities from being tracked across multiple services. It will also prevent anyone from viewing your browsing history should you lose your mobile device. Doing this is relatively easy by following the steps outlined in the "**Securing your Smartphone**" section in the appendix.

Secure Disposal:

When you eventually tire of your smartphone and upgrade to the latest model, be careful of how you dispose of your old mobile device. Since this device contains much of your personal information, be sure to perform a factory reset before selling your mobile device on Craigslist, eBay, or donating it to charity. You can bring your phone to your cellular service provider and they will be happy to assist you.

Unless you take steps to protect your privacy, anyone who receives your discarded mobile device could access your personal and financial information. If your mobile device has a mico-SDcard or removable memory, be sure to remove this before discarding your phone. If you are concerned about your ability to scrub your smartphone clean, there is always the trusty hammer method. This method is 100% reliable, not to mention a lot of fun.

By this point, the security and privacy settings of your cellphone/smartphone have been tightened up and you now have increased your awareness of the privacy implications of the device you spend more quality time with than your own partner.

It's now a good time to move on to the next step of this adventure and secure that other device that may be betraying your privacy – your computer.

Securing your Laptop/Computer:

Your personal computer, be it a laptop or a desktop, contains some of your most sensitive information and could be viewed as an external backup device for your brain. It will likely contain your identity, your tax records, your homework, your web browsing habits, chat logs, your login credentials to Facebook, Amazon and eBay and other websites. It contains your personal papers and perhaps your journal – detailing your private life as well as your hopes and dreams. But is it secure?

You cannot tell by looking at it so put on your geek hat, ensure the propeller is functional, and get started securing your platform. I will warn you now – this is the most technical part of the book so please bear with me. It's not too bad.

Before we talk about securing your on-line activities we have to make sure your personal computer has not already been tampered with or otherwise compromised. What would be the point of securing your online activities if your personal computer is already betraying you?

You can restore your trust by following these five easy steps...

Step 1:

Download and install anti-virus/anti-malware security software. If you have high speed Internet, contact your service provider and see if they have security software available for free. Comcast and Charter offers free security software with your account. If your service provider does not offer free anti-virus/security software (and there's really no reason why they shouldn't), you can find free anti-virus software online. MalwareBytes, AVG, and Avast! are all excellent products (at the time of this writing.)

Step 2:

After installing the security software, update the software and security signatures.

Step 3:

Run a full scan. This could take awhile, depending on your system, so you might want to find something to do in the meantime. Just don't do it on the computer that you are scanning.

Step 4:

If the security scans detect any problems – allow the software to "fix" your computer automatically and clean out the threats. Then reboot your system.

Step 5:

Run the scan again. Repeat these steps until the security software reports that your computer is clean. Remember, it may still have a problem because these scans are not 100% accurate but you are in a much better place now.

Login/Username:

On your personal computer make sure your account does not have administrative privileges. This is because should an application, say your web browser, misbehave it will limit the impact and scope of any subsequent security breach that may occur. If you suspect a security breach, or witness some unusual behaviors on your computer, immediately repeat the steps 1-5 and make sure your computer has not been compromised.

As with your smartphone, make sure you have the screen lock enabled and a secure code used to unlock and access your system. What you have learned in securing your mobile device can be applied to your personal computer. This will help prevent access in the event - however likely – you lose control of your laptop or your desktop system is stolen.

If you want to be really sure of securing your system, use a BIOS password and a Hard Drive password. To set up the BIOS/Hard Drive password you can follow these steps:

BIOS/Hard Drive Password:

Turn on or reboot your computer. The screen will display a series of information.

A message like: "Hit the <DEL> key to enter the BIOS setup program" will appear."

When you do hit DEL at the right time you'll see a menu displayed. This is your BIOS.

Go to the Security portion of the menu and select what password you wish to use to protect your system. It's non-trivial to bypass this password, so make sure you never lose or forget it. If you set your hard drive password, be aware that it will likely be impossible to access your system in the event that your password is forgotten.

Securing Your Software:

Now that your system is "secured", you can now begin locking down your individual applications. The applications that are the most dangerous to your identity and privacy are your Web Browser and your Email Client. By default, these two software packages are not configured to protect your privacy, rather they are configured for ease of use and for the benefit of online advertising. By following these steps you can improve your on-line security and privacy without sacrificing your on-line experience.

Web Browsers:

Browsing the web is the primary reason most people get their computers. The greatest threats to your online privacy are your browsing history and the management of cookies. Your browsing history is a record of every website you have visited that has been automatically stored in your user profile.

There is really no purpose to keep this information. If you visit a website that you find informative, you can always opt to "bookmark" the page. That way you can return to the website whenever you need to.

A good practice is to clear your browsing history and to configure your web browser to not remember the websites you have visited. Clearing the history now can help you avoid that annoying reminder that you once misspelled "clock" when searching for a new timepiece.

Cookies are little pieces of information that a website will place on your computer when you view a page. The websites can then retrieve this information and use it to track you across the Internet. Cookies are useful during a session and some web applications will not work without them. However, once they are no longer required, they should be purged from your system.

Many software packages will offer to install a toolbar. Don't. If you have a browser toolbar installed, consider removing it. When you use a toolbar, your search queries and other online activities, can be tracked and reported to the publisher.

To better protect your privacy when surfing the net, you can configure your web browser in a few easy steps outlined in the appendix "**Privacy Enabled Browsing**".

Privacy enabled browsing allows you to surf the internet without leaving any breadcrumbs behind and will help prevent websites from tracking your online activities.

Email Clients:

The next thing to do is to configure your email to display your email as "plain text". What you are reading now is plain text. What you view on a web page is HTML.

Email in HTML format is not bad but it does present a risk to your security and privacy. If someone you have met online sends you a link to view their photos on the dating site you are subscribed to, you might have no problem clicking the link to view their pictures. You're curious so you click the link and the dating website pops up and you attempt to log in. What may have happened is known as a "phishing" attack.

The link they have sent you is not from the dating website, but rather from a system that they control that is set up to impersonate the dating site. When you enter your login information, the fake website then forwards the request to the real website only now this stranger has your login information as well as full access to your account on the legitimate site. This scenario has happened to a friend of mine recently and it had caused her a lot of grief in a very short time. If your email client flags any email as an attack – believe it – and do not click the link.

Another risk in viewing e-mail in HTML format is what is known as a "web bug". A web-bug is any piece of information that can automatically be loaded from a remote location when viewing the email. If you had HTML enabled in your e-mail client and someone sends you an email containing one of these little treasures, when you open the email, your computer could reach back through the Internet and try to pull that piece of information back onto your system without your knowledge. When you open your email and this occurs, the system serving up the web bug will know when you read your email, and the IP address of your computer's network – which could be your home.

To be safe, it's best to only view your emails in plain text. If you trust the source of the email, you can always click, the "show remote images" button. To configure your email client to better protect your privacy, visit the appendix section on "**Email Privacy**"

Securing Your Home Network:

If you have high speed internet at your house, you likely also use a wireless router to connect your laptops, smartphones, and tablets and nowadays, your television, to the Internet. With your developing sense of privacy awareness you might want to double check and ensure the security of your home network.

Your wireless router has a unique identifier known as the Service Set Identifier (SSID). On your wireless router, make sure that your SSID does not contain any usable information. Some people set their SSID to things ranging from their name, street address, apartment number to their home phone number. If your wireless router is configured with a SSID that has any identifiable information, then it would be a good idea to change it to something more secure.

If the SSID is set to your pet's or child's name, or manufacturer, change it so something neutral like "myWiFi". If you are very concerned about privacy, consider disabling the broadcast of your Wi-Fi SSID entirely. To do this, you will have to go online and download the user manual for your device and follow the instructions.

You can also "opt-out" of Google's Wi-Fi location-based service database by appending "_nomap" to the SSID of your wireless router. When you connect to the Internet and use Google, or other company's services, the SSID can be captured and sent to the service provider revealing your physical location as you use the Internet. Once you set the SSID on your wireless router to "myWiFi_nomap", then, according to Google: "The next time a user's device sends information about your Wi-Fi access point to the Google Location Server through a reliable channel, our system will note the _nomap tag and remove the access point from our Location Server after it is processed."... however long that takes.

There will be some location information revealed anytime you use the Internet. If your computer is plugged into your router with a cable, you are still revealing the IP address that your service provider supplied you and that IP address may provide rough physical location information. If you wish to hide that IP address from the websites you visit, you can consider using an anonymizer or "Onion Routing" as it's called, to better secure your communications. Information about this security and privacy technique can be found on: **www.torproject.org**

While you are digging around your wireless router, you should also verify that the administrator password has been set. If you are able to log into your wireless router without a password, then anyone on your home network can reconfigure your router without your knowledge or permission.

To test this, connect an Ethernet cable directly into your wireless router and then, using your newly secured browser and go to this address:

https://192.168.0.1

or..

https://192.168.1.1

Try to log in using blank, “admin”and “administrator” as user names with either a blank password or “admin” as the password. Happy hacking!

How did I know your the address of the device in your private home? This is because your router has a presence in two worlds: The External world and the Internal world.

The External world is the evil Internet. If you had directly connected your computer to the Internet, your computer would likely be attacked by automated hacking tools within a few minutes. The router provides a firewall, or a protective barrier, between your safe internal network and the Wild West.

Your Internal network is the network in your home or business and systems within this network are shielded from the external network by your Firewall. The address to your router mentioned earlier is the Internal address to the device, by default. *(Note: If these do not work, then you will need to check the owners manual for the correct address.)*

If you did not personally set up your wireless router, then you should verify that the following safety features have been set up properly:

Administrator Password:

Change it to a secure password.
This prevents anyone from changing the configuration of your router without the proper credentials.

Administrative Access:

- Limit access to "wired" and not "wireless".
- Restrict access to HTTPS.

This prevents anyone with wireless access to attempt to reconfigure your router and HTTPS prevents anyone with a "sniffer" from stealing the password over the air or across the network.

Wireless Network Name (SSID):

- No identifiable information
- No names/pet's name/address, etc.)
- Append "_nomap"

This prevents identifying the router as *your* router or its physical location. Note: if you are very concerned, you an opt not to broadcast your SSID.

<u>**VERY IMPORTANT!**</u>

Wireless Security: Use WPA2 and a strong password.

This prevents unauthorized uses from accessing your wireless network and the computers in your home. If wireless security is disabled, then anyone that receives your Wi-Fi signal would be able to use your network to access the Internet.

They can be your neighbor or some creep sitting in their car outside your home who's downloading child pornography or sending threatening emails to the President. When the authorities investigate, they could track the source to your home and you could be falsely identified as the perpetrator and get a nice little visit by stern official types with guns and badges.

It's an easy fix and not worth the risks of hosting an open, unsecured, Wi-Fi network. Write down the new access password as your laptop, smartphone, and tablets will now require this information the next time they attempt to connect to your network. Do not use the WEP option as it can easily be hacked using publicly available cracking tools.

Wireless MAC Filter:

If you are very concerned about security and privacy, consider enabling wireless MAC filter along with the WPA2 security.

This will restrict access to your wireless network to only those devices who have both the correct MAC address and the correct WPA2 password. This is much more secure and only a little more inconvenient.

Refresh Your IP Address:

To connect to the Internet you will be provided with an IP address by your service provider. Most of the Internet providers will dynamically assign you an IP address from a pool of IP addresses that they currently control.

Anyone on the Internet will be able poke at that IP address and, if your network is misconfigured or you have a computer connected directly to the Internet, your systems will be subjected to constant hacker attacks. Your IP address could also potentially reveal your physical location.

Since all of your on-line activities are being logged somewhere, and services that have access to your physical location and have your IP address, they can now associate that IP address with your physical location and, depending on the privacy policies, share that association with other companies.

To help prevent this, periodically turn off your Internet router, or cable modem. If you go away for the weekend, turn it off. When you turn off your cable modem for an extended period, the IP address that you were using can be returned to the address pool and will be acquired by someone else. When your return from your refreshing mini-vacation and turn on your cable-modem, you will be assigned a new IP address by your provider. If you want to take matters into your own hands and get a new address yourself, call your Internet service provider and ask them for a new IP address.

Before You Go Online:

Your Online Identities:

Most websites now use your email address for login (Google, Facebook, LinkedIn) and therefore, you will need to create and maintain several on-line identities. Each of these separate identities will act a buffer between your real world activities and those conducted on line. You can have as many online identities as you are comfortable managing, after all – they're free. The identities that you will obtain and deploy as part of your privacy protection plan will each fall into one of three roles. These roles are:

Personal:

Your real email address. This address is only used for email to your friends, family and business. Configure with your first name only. If this account is compromised and you are forced to change your email address, you will have to let your friends and family know of the change.

This is the identity that you will guard and be very careful to not disclose to people you do not know and trust. Think of this as your "clean" email address.

Online:

If you use Amazon or any other of the online retailers – use this email address. If this identity is compromised, then you would have to change the email addresses on each of the websites that you conduct your business on. If you are very concerned about your privacy, then have a separate email identity for each of the businesses on which you have an account. This would make managing your on-line purchases much easier to track as each identity in your email folder will only have the activity for that single online business. Think of this as your "grey" email address.

Throwaway:

This is your garbage identity. This is the email address that you can use on on-line dating sites and sites you do not know or trust. This email address can be handed to people you have just met and do not yet trust and can be used to sign up for "Special offers" and those sorts of things. Think of this as your "dirty" email address.

This identity should be set up in such a way as to contain absolutely zero personal information. The contents of the email to and from this identity should also not contain any identifiable information. If you accidentally sent or receive an email with any personal information with this account, then you should immediately delete the email message. If this identity is compromised, just toss it, get another throwaway email address and start over.

Each of these identities will need a password to access them. Make absolutely certain that you do not share your password with any other of your identities and employ good password security.

Password Security:

Clifford Stoll, the author of "The Cuckoo's Egg", a book detailing his exploits of chasing a hacker though cyberspace, has a very apt saying regarding password security:

"Your password is like your toothbrush – change it every few months and never share it with anyone." - Clifford Stoll

You could also add... *"...or any other service"*.

Do not use the same password on multiple systems. If you share a common password across multiple services, then when and if one of these services get hacked and your password is compromised, the hackers have access to all of the other services you use.

"But why would hackers care about me?"

They don't. What the hackers care about is access and your login information is valuable to them as it will provide them with access to the services you use and the ability to impersonate you.

While pretending to be you, the hackers will have access to your personal account information and can hide as you while they attempt to hack the website. If they succeed, and are able to elevate their security level or obtain credit card and personal information of other users, they will do so as you.

There is a vibrant, underground, black market in the hacker world where groups of these people trade electronic identities. While your specific identity is not valuable, it will likely be bundled up with a collection of other identities and sold/traded on this black market.

By not sharing your login information and passwords across multiple services, you can minimize the impact of a security breach in one service from spilling over to the other services you use and can help save yourself a lot of headaches in the future. It's a little more inconvenient but the protection this affords is well worth the effort.

"But, how will I remember all of those passwords?"

It is very easy....

First, choose a reasonably strong password.

For example: "**1LuvMyD0g!**"

Consider this to be your base password. If you incorporate the information on where your account is used, it will be much easier to remember.

For example:

Amazon.com:

> "1LuvMyD0g!**am4z**" or "**book**1LuvMyD0g!" or "1LuvMyD0g!**@amz**"

eBay.com:

> "1LuvMyD0g!**eb4y**" or "1LuvMyD0g!**bid**" or "1LuvMyD0g!**@eBay**"

Facebook.com:

> "1LuvMyD0g!**fb00k**" or "**Fb**1LuvMyD0g!**ook**" or "1LuvMyD0g!**@fbk**"

The key is to be consistent in how you apply the website information into your base password. The purpose of having a different password for each of your on-line accounts and identities is in the event there is a security breach and one of your user identities is compromised, the attacker will not be able to access all of your other accounts.

If you had used the same password on all of your accounts and had the misfortune to fall victim to that dating site phishing attack described earlier, then whoever has your credentials now has access to all your emails, and from your emails knows what other accounts you use and can then try to access those accounts. Not only could this embarrass you, but they can also have access to your financial related information and cause you financial harm.

Practice Safe Computing:

Your laptop computer can be thought of as a big clunky smartphone that you also use to produce "TPS reports" and file your taxes on. This device will likely contain more of your sensitive information than your mobile device so, like your smartphone, you need to be careful with how you use it.

Software:

There is currently an arms race underway between the hackers and the security community so be sure that all of your software is current and up to date. By running older software, you increase your chances of falling victim to a hack attack so make sure that your operating system, applications, and security software are all current and up to date. The software vendors make this very easy to do so double check and make sure that automatic updates are enabled.

Email:

Be wary of any links you see in any email you receive. As we've seen, if you click on a malicious link, you might fall victim to a phishing attack and could lose your login credentials or bank account information.

A legitimate email will never request that you enter your login or account information – ever. If you receive an email of this type, forward the email to the FTC at **spam@uce.gov** and then delete it. Another email threat are emails that contain attachments. These can be tricky in that they can appear to be legitimate and from the post office, or UPS, claiming you have received a package and contain an attachment of your order.

If you look at the attachment it will likely be named something reasonable like "Invoice" and if you have downloaded the attachment, it will look like a document file. If you click on the "document", it could infect your computer with a virus or malware. If you have your security software installed, this makes it much more difficult to do, so before you save or open any attachment, be sure the run it through your security software first.

It will also help if you use a little common sense when looking at these types of email. If the email states something like "Your flight confirmation" and email appears to be from US Air, look at the address list. If you see that 1,000 people have also received the same flight confirmation, then either US Air has seriously overbooked that flight, or the message is a scam and is trying to infect your computer. Be sure to forward the email to: **spam@uce.gov** before deleting it.

By forwarding all of your spam and malicious email to the Federal Trade Commission, you are helping them help you by gathering malicious email statistics and providing raw data for their research efforts.

When you forward an email from another source, be sure to remove all of the email addresses of people in the original email. These people have no idea that their email address has been disclosed to unknown people and they may not be comfortable with that fact.

Several years ago a friend forwarded me an email and I noticed it contained the personal email address for the actress Jennifer Connelly. No, I didn't do that.. or that.. I simply respected her privacy and deleted it. I felt she would not appreciate the fact that her private email address was sent to some random guy in Massachusetts. *It was kind of cool though.*

When sending email to a large group of people, always use the Blind Carbon Copy, or BCC, feature in your email program. If you simply send an email to a large number of email addresses, then everyone receiving the email will also be able to see the email addresses of all the other recipients. If you use the BCC feature, then only the sender's and your own email addresses are displayed.

Software Downloads:

Treat any software you download from the Internet as a potential risk. If you download anything, make sure that the application has been scanned by your installed security software before you attempt to install it.

Some of the security software will automatically scan the file immediately after it is downloaded but be double sure and run a manual scan yourself using a different anti-virus package. This will help prevent your systems from being infected with a virus, malware, or spyware.

Plan On Having Your Laptop Stolen:

As with your smartphone, you have to assume that you will lose control of your laptop computer at some point in time. It doesn't take much, which is why you have to take precautionary measures to ensure the physical security of your device. Do not leave it unattended in your car or on a table in a cafe when you go to use the restroom. Ask yourself the same question you did with your smartphone:

"If I knew I would lose my laptop tomorrow to my worst enemy, what would I do today?"

Assume you will have your laptop stolen and act now...

Step 1:

Search your system for any sensitive or personally identifiable information. Anything that could harm you if your system fell into the wrong hands should be protected. This includes Names, Account numbers, SSN and other financial information.

Step 2:

Encrypt all sensitive files and keep that data in an encrypted folder. An encrypted folder will provide you a place on your desktop where you can drag-and-drop files you consider worthy of protection.

These files can include, resumes, tax returns, bank statements, medical records and photos. When you need to access your data in the future, you'll be prompted to enter a password. Make the password secure by using the techniques described earlier, using a base password with the service name.

Setting up an encrypted folder is very easy to do and should only take a few minutes of your time. The detailed steps can be found in the appendix under "**File Encryption**".

Step 3:

Important: Do not leave unencrypted copies of your sensitive files on your system. If you took the time to secure your documents, it will not help you if you have unsecured copies anywhere on your computer. The best policy is to:

Decrypt Document → Perform Your Work → Encrypt Document → Backup

Leaving unencrypted sensitive files on your system after encrypting them, is like locking the doors of your convertible when the top is down.

Take Out the Trash:

When you delete files on your computer the files are not immediately removed from your system. Instead of deleting your files, your system has moved the files into a "Trash" or "Recycle Bin" where they will sit until you empty the trash. Anyone with access to your system will be able to retrieve your deleted files so be sure to frequently take out the trash.

Even after you take out the trash, your files can still be retrieved using any freely available file recovery tool. If you want to prevent anyone from recovering your deleted files, you can install a "secure erase" utility that will overwrite your "deleted" files and prevent their recovery.

On Mac computers, you can securely empty your trash by clicking on **Finder > Secure Empty Trash**.

On Windows machines, download and install the free software package "Erasure" found at **http://eraser.heidi.ie/**

Beware of Unknown Media:

Hackers in the past have sprinkled USB drives and SDcards, used in digital cameras, in parking lots outside of secured government installations and have compromised some of their systems.

Someone could give you a USB drive or SDcard to show you their photos, but, without your knowledge, install a key-logger / backdoor onto your system. Once installed, this person can then remotely spy on your entire computer and watch you as you type an email to your friends.

The best policy is to have a secured computer and to scan any portable media before accessing its contents with your laptop or other system.

SSL Everywhere:

When using your computer to browse the web, always try to secure your online activities by using SSL/HTTPS. If you are sitting at a cafe and log into Facebook, the default setting at the time of this writing is that your Facebook session is not fully protected. Anyone in your area using the FireSheep software package could hijack your session and compromise your Facebook account.

Firesheep is a free Firefox/Chrome browser add-on that's designed to take over the communication session between your computer/smartphone and the website you have logged into. Once your session is stolen, the snoop will have full access to your account and will be able to impersonate you online.

To prevent this, consider installing the security package "HTTPS everywhere" which can be found on the Electronic Frontier Foundation's website:

https://www.eff.org/https-everywhere

This package is easy to install and will secure all of your online web sessions against snooping and session hijacking.

When attempting to login to, or pull your email from, an online server, and your web browser/mail client displays a security warning – believe it. This could indicate that you have connected to a rogue access point that is attempting to execute a man-in-the-middle attack and steal your credentials.

If this happens, shut off your computer and use your smartphone with the **Wi-Fi turned off,** to get your email; this will force your smartphone to use the cellular data service.

Note: This is not 100% secure because micro-cell towers can be used to intercept your cellular data communications, so always make sure that your mobile applications employ SSL/TLS security.

All online service providers that are entrusted with your login information should have the entire session protected by SSL. Since most do not, you can better protect your online activities by configuring your system to securely access the Internet.

Secure Backup:

Always back up your computer. I've personally been burned by this too many times, so I have multiple, encrypted backups of my important files on multiple media.

The key is to not only back up your important data, but to also secure it with encryption and a strong password. There are many online backup service offerings like iCloud, Mozy and Dropbox, that provide a convenient way to backup and restore your data.

These services do offer security and encryption, but there is really no way for you to be sure if the service is living up to their promises. You can make sure by only using these online backup services on files that you have encrypted yourself.

That way, if the online backup service suffers a security breach, your information will be protected by the security precautions you know you have performed yourself.

Secure Disposal:

When you eventually want to upgrade to a newer computer, be careful with how you dispose of your old system. Since this device contains your most sensitive personal information, be sure to back up your important files and scrub any personal information from your old system before you sell or give it away.

If you are planning on recycling your old computer, you can remove the hard drives and reenact that scene from Office Space and smash them a few times on a hard surface before sending them off - just make sure you have backed up your files first.

When you sell or donate your old system, you might think that you can delete your personal files and hand your system over to the new owner; but this is not safe. Deleted files are easily recovered using a variety of free tools so it is best to completely wipe the system clean before handing it over.

The easiest way is to bring your system to BestBuy, Staples, or a computer repair shop and tell them you are selling your computer and need to wipe the disk and perform a system restore. They will know what to do but be sure to get a price quote first.

If you want to do this yourself, the first step to make a backup copy of all of your important files as this process is not reversible.

Then get a copy of your original installation disk that came with your computer. Many manufacturers place a copy of your installation disk on your system disk so you will have to look in your owners manual or go online for directions on creating an installation disk.

If you have created your own installation disk, verify that it works by using the disk to boot your computer. If your computer does not boot, then you will need to repeat the steps to creating an installation disk or get some assistance because you will need a working installation disk before proceeding to the next step.

At this point you have backed up your important files and have a working installation disk. Go online a search for "secure erase" and download and install the secure erase software package onto your computer.

Now you can run the disk wipe software and it will securely delete your entire system. This may take a long time as your entire hard drive is being scrubbed of your personal information.

After your system has been purged, use your installation disk and reinstall the operating system. It is very easy to do, just put the installation disk in, reboot your system, and the installation program will guide you though the entire process.

For any portable media (USB flash drives, Camera cards, external hard drives) that may contain personal information, be sure to securely delete the entire device before discarding them.

Webcams:

Webcams are often used in chat applications and are a great way to stay in touch with people who live far away or right down the hall. If you do use a webcam, make sure it's unplugged or covered up after each use. You cannot tell just by looking at it if it's on, so be certain to unplug it or turn it away when it is not needed. You can also take a Post-It note and trim a little sticky piece and place it over the camera lens on your laptop.

The reason for this precaution is there's a large number of software packages out there than can be installed on your system that have the ability to spy on your computer as well as remotely turn on your camera. If you are uncomfortable with this possibility, you can simply cover up your webcam until you need it.

Online Privacy Profile:

Now that your smartphone, computing devices, and network have been scrubbed and their integrity reasonably verified – I say "reasonably" because you can never be 100% sure – now you can open the can of worms that might be your online presence.

When you are ready, you can begin the short journey to self discovery and enlightenment by becoming your own stalker. Why not? If you are trying to protect yourself from cyberstalking, why not cyberstalk yourself? It's fun to see what information about you is out there. *Wait. Did I say fun? It's actually a little unnerving.*

You can begin stalking yourself by entering the following queries into a variety of search engines. (*Note: make sure you're not already logged into any of them as the search will be tied to the user account you have logged in with.*)

Conduct the following searches:

1) Full Name (First & Last Name - with and without quotes)
Example: **"Betty Boop"** and **Betty Boop**

2) All of the email addresses you have used:
boopdedoop@yahoo.com

3) All of the phone numbers you have used:
413-555-2525

Click on each of the links and make notes on what information is published and what sites are presenting your information.

Now do the same thing using other search engines (Google, Bing, Dogpile, etc.)

This is how you appear to the anonymous world – that is, anyone on the planet with a computer and an Internet connection, over 2.6 billion people, can see this information about you.

At this point you have your online privacy profile. If you are like most people, there were quite a few surprises in the report and may have found this exercise a bit unsettling.

The search results can be divided into several categories:

Social Media Results:

Search results from social media sites will likely be at the top of your query results. Facebook, LinkedIn, Myspace...

By clicking on the Facebook and LinkedIn, other social media links, you can verify that your privacy setting for those services are correct.

If you find that your profile has been misconfigured and you are exposing too much of your information to the world, then visit each of the sites that you have accounts on and adjust your profile privacy settings accordingly.

After you have adjusted your account privacy settings, be sure to follow the directions outlined in the "**Removing Links from Search Engines**" section.

Public record search results will likely be the next set of links in your query results page - and this is where it can get interesting.

Public Records Search Results:

Interstate data brokers, as defined by Personal Data Privacy and Security Act of 2009, are "business entities which, for monetary fees or dues, regularly engage in the practice of collecting, transmitting, or providing access to sensitive personally identifiable information on more than 5,000 individuals to non-affiliated third parties on an interstate basis."

The results generated from these online information brokers will likely contain your full name, your age, current address, the name(s) of your children and possibly the name and location of your other family members. If you click on one of those links, you will see offers to join their service and can view your personal information – as well as the information on other people.

From MyLife.com website: *"Finding* ***Jane Q Public*** *is at your fingertips, with* **MyLife.com***'s ability to locate even the hardest to find people from* **Northampton,** *Massachusetts!"*

What I find interesting is the fact that if a corporation had used a photo of me without my permission for a product we'll call "Uncle Al's Hemorrhoid Cream", after I came out of hiding, I could sue the corporation for using my likeness without my permission. But, if you Google your name, then clicked on the links presented by these data brokers, you will see that they are marketing their services to you by using your own personal information!

The ease and availability of public records can facilitate violence – especially against women. If someone wanted to get to you in the physical world – the public records search results make it trivial to do so.

This is not intentional - but is what social scientists call an "unintended consequence" of making too much personal information publicly available. Anyone with access to the Internet can use these services to obtain the physical location of any person who has not made a conscious effort to protect her or his privacy.

If you read the marketing materials provided by these public records corporations, they will paint a happy picture of unicorns and rainbows where lost loved ones are reunited or perhaps, an old love is rekindled and the happy couple walks into the fading light – hand in hand.

But the reality is, the disclosure of your public information to anonymous people is a known threat to your personal safety. The state of California has known the risks since 1999 and passed the "Safe at Home" privacy protection laws. This law helps protect the privacy of survivors of domestic abuse, stalking, and sexual assault, as well as reproductive health care professionals and their patients.

Their FAQ specifically mentions public records search:

From http://www.sos.ca.gov/safeathome/sah-faqs3.html, on March 2012. *Sections 6205-6210 of the California Government Code, protects victims of domestic violence and sexual assault.*

"Many of these victims are forced to go into hiding because they fear being tracked down by their abusers, assailants or stalkers through voter, school, telephone, utilities or drivers license records. ***With the availability of personal information on the Internet and through public records searches, there is a real danger facing victims with determined stalkers.****"*

What troubles me is why does anyone have to wait until their very lives are endangered before a law will kick in and protect their privacy from being violated by public records search queries?

You would probably not know your life was in danger, until your life actually was - in danger.

So, why not err on the side of caution? And, it's not just you, anyone who has not protected their privacy is vulnerable.

In 2005, a Federal Judge came home to find her husband and mother had been brutally murdered. During the investigation, it was discovered that the door had been forced open. Evidence presented during the trial included an email that the suspect sent, asking for the Judge's home address. Some time later, a message, posted on a hate group website, published the Judge's home address.

Her family was murdered soon after.

The question that no one has addressed in any of the news reports is this: How did they get the Judge's home address?

It's out there...

Public information on members of Law Enforcement and other members of the Court is currently sitting in the databases of online data brokers. If you are a Judge, and you want to protect yourself and your family, you would have to call up each of these data brokers and ask, "Would you please remove my personal information from your systems."

Taken from the public link privacylock.ussearch.com in Mar 2012:

"In order for us to process your request, we need to verify your identity. Proof of identity can be a state issued ID card or driver's license. We will only use this information to process your request. No request will be processed without complete information and verification of identity.

Requests for opt out will not be processed over the phone or via email. Subject to limited exceptions for elected officials and/or law enforcement officers, *US Search does not process any third party requests or requests submitted in any other manner."*

When a Judges and Police Officers contact these information brokers to remove their personal information – they are forced to reveal the fact they are Judges and Police Officers. Anyone at these information brokers with access to the systems containing this information could then compile a list of Police and Judges and then sell that information on the black market – all without the knowledge the information broker.

All it would take is physical access, a little ingenuity and a USB stick or camera phone.

If Judges are vulnerable, what chance does a private citizen have in protecting her or his privacy from disclosure?

Public records search results are a stalker's paradise. If you have purchased a home or voted, or ever appeared in the phone book, you will be in the public records database and any search engine query will generate your Name, Age, Street address and Phone number and even your relatives.

You need to ask yourself how comfortable you are with the availability of this information to anonymous queries. The electronic dissemination of public records is one of the biggest threats to your personal privacy and in some cases, your personal safety.

These data brokers will sell public information they have collected to anyone. What happens when these brokers sell public records to a business interest that then exports the data outside the United States and into another country? Exporting the public information of US citizens to foreign countries is easy when you consider that fact that the public records - Name, Address, SSN, Phone numbers(s) - for every adult in this country is small enough to fit on a USB stick.

Unfortunately, this is already happening. One example is the website "American Yellow Pages" (**www.ypstate.com**), which is a system sitting in China that is hosting the exported public records of American citizens.

Since your public records have been exported outside of the United States, there is now nothing you can do legally about having your data removed from that server. The United States laws do not apply there and our government does not have any authority on foreign soil where your data is now residing.

If you find your US Public Records are sitting on a foreign server, you can attempt to have them purge your information by contacting the website operators asking them to remove your data from their systems. But they don't have to. You can also request the search engines remove the links from their search results – or better yet – completely ban those sites.

This is why it's so important to rein in disclosure of public records – because once your data has been published – it's gone.

If you are uncomfortable with the availability of your public information, then you can do something right now to take matters into your own hands and "Opt-Out" and regain some control of your privacy.

One way is if you wish to go the Cadillac route: Hire a lawyer and drop this whole mess in their lap. Your attorney can file take-down notices and opt-out requests with each of the websites that is displaying your information. It will cost more, but it'll be very convenient for you do.

There are for-profit companies that claim they can remove your public record information for a fee.

For most of us, we will have to brown bag it and do it ourselves - Here's an example of how:

This exercise will probably take an entire afternoon. There are detailed instructions for contacting these Public Information Brokers and "opting out" on the following privacy related websites. Contact them and search for the magic words: "opt-out" or go to these links.

www.privacyrights.org/node/1448
www.worldprivacyforum.org/toptenoptout.html
www.unlistmy.info

Opt-Out Walk-Through:

Here's what it's like to remove your information from a few of these search engines. Responsible public information brokers will provide you a quick, easy way to "opt out" and will remove your identity from their systems within 72 hours.

Before you begin, take a photograph of your state issued driver license and then, using a graphic editor like "paint", "Paintbrush", or "Gimp", and block out your image, the license number and your signature. Save this modified image to "opt-out.jpg" as you will be needing this later.

Mylife.com:

www.mylife.com is a hybrid service provider that combines elements of both Public Records Search and Social Media and attempts to lure you into joining by offering to inform you "Who's been searching for you".

On their landing page you may see your name, your age, and the name of any children and other family members.

If you are uncomfortable with the information that MyLife is reporting on you then take back control and Opt-out.

Mylife will offer to let you login using your Facebook, LinkedIn, or Twitter account. Don't. The fastest way to remove your information is to call customer service

Call the MyLife toll free number (888)-704-1900 and tell them you want opt-out and have your information removed from their systems and be sure to ask for a confirmation number. Their call center is open 24 hours a day and they will be happy to help you out.

Whitepages.com:

Whitepages.com offers an easy way to have your information removed from their database. Go to their website: **www.whitepages.com** and enter your information. At the bottom of the page is a link that asks: "Is this you? Remove your listing". Enter the Captcha code and you're done!

Intelius.com:

Intelius offers an online opt-out form and is responsive to requests to remove records from their search engine results. This service is also feeds the results of other public records search engines and so by removing your information from Intelius, you will have removed your information from other public information websites as well. You have to be sure to verify that your information has been removed once you have opted-out of Intelius. Go to:

https://www.intelius.com/optout.php

Fill out the opt-put form and upload that photograph of your license that you had prepared earlier. Intelius will remove your information promptly and send you confirmation to the email address you have supplied. (Be sure to use one of your dirty email addresses).

Other public information brokers are less helpful when you attempt to protect yourself.

Taken from http://www.zabasearch.com/block_records/ on Mar 2012:

"In order for ZabaSearch to "opt out" your public information from being viewable on the ZabaSearch website, we need to verify your identity and require faxed proof of identity. Proof of identity can be a state issued ID card or driver's license. If you are faxing a copy of your driver's license, cross out the photo and the driver's license number. We only need to see the name, address and date of birth. We will only use this information to process your opt out request. Please fax to 425-974-6194 and allow 4 to 6 weeks to process your request."

It will take 4 to 6 weeks to hide your own information and you have to divulge your identity to an organization you did not authorize the use of your information in the first place.

Another example is **www.instantcheckmate.com**. If your public information is on this site and you wish to have it removed, you have two choices. (Mar 2012)

1) Put all of your information (First Name, Last Name, Date of Birth, Address, City, State, Zip) on a card and send to their headquarters and they will process your request in **2-4 weeks.**

2) Give them your identity (First Name, Last Name, Date of Birth, Address, City, State, Zip) and your credit card and **pay $4.95** to have it removed expeditiously.

Seems pretty unreasonable to me when other information brokers provide an online "opt-out" without requiring you to pay a fee or disclose any additional information.

LexisNexis.com: Will allow you the option to opt-out if you are at substantial risk of physical harm.

From: http://www.lexisnexis.com/privacy/for-consumers/opt-out-of-lexisnexis.aspx, March 2012

"Documentation Required for Opt-Out Request

Each opt-out request must include documentation substantiating the risk of physical harm or the individual's status as an identity theft victim or as a person otherwise meeting the above criteria. LexisNexis reserves the right to determine in its sole reasonable discretion what documentation meets the above criteria. If your opt-out request is not approved we will promptly inform you about that determination.

- *If you are a law enforcement officer or public official, submit a letter from your supervisor stating that your position exposes you to a threat of death or serious bodily harm; or*
- *If you are a victim of identity theft, submit a copy of a police report documenting the identity theft or documentation that verifies the identity theft claim such as a letter from your credit card company, and an Identity Theft Affidavit; or*
- *If you are at risk of physical harm but do not work in law enforcement, submit a copy of a court protective order, a copy of a police report or similar documentation such as a letter from a social worker, a shelter administrator or a health care professional"*

If you had a protective order, a police report, or a letter from a health care professional, then it is likely you have already suffered a traumatic event. Your information has already been published and having Lexis-Nexis remove it after the fact would be of little benefit to you.

As mentioned earlier, you would probably not know your life was in danger, until your life actually was in danger so why do some these companies make it difficult for you to protect your privacy before you are actually subjected to physical harm?

Some public record search engines will make it very difficult for you to remove your information. They will have broken links in the "opt-out" page, or the phone number you are referred to will never pick up. I would be willing to bet that the credit-card payment link is up 100% of the time, but for some reason, the opt-out link is sometimes broken. If you find broken opt-out link, an unresponsive phone number, or a surly customer support representative, file a complaint against the company with the Federal Trade Commission at :

www.ftccomplaintassistant.gov

Include as much information as you can about what happened and, if possible, let the company know you have filed a complaint against them. Then wait a few days and try again to remove your information from their site. The problem might have magically been fixed by then.

Post Office Box:

Another strategy to help protect your physical self would be for you to obtain a post-office box, either in your town, or any other town, depending on the size of the buffer you wish to create. Then contact all of the public record search engines and submit a request to update your information.

Public record search engines will be more than happy to assist you and allow you to update your information for free. Some make it difficult to remove your information but most will be very helpful in allowing you to help improve the accuracy of their products and services.

After you obtain your post-office box, begin updating every account you have and have all of your physical mail go there. You can think of this as your "Dirty" address and your home address your "Clean" address.

Then go to your county clerk's office and ask to review your public records. Ask the clerk's office how you can go about changing your public records. Your county clerk should allow you review your public records and allow you to update your address to your new P.O. Box. Online information brokers will then acquire your updated information and subsequent public records search queries will generate your PO box and not your home address.

These examples are a good start. For complete coverage, you would need to contact every public search engine that your information shows up in and demand that they remove your private information or pay and use a service to do this on your behalf – but be aware that now that service has your personal information. It's a bit of a pain to do yourself, but it could help keep the creepers out of your life and should only take a few hours of your time.

Public Record Laws:

After you have purged your public information from these public record search engines, the next thing to do is to **contact your lawmakers** and inform them of your privacy concerns and ask them to work to change the public records laws. Seriously. The current public records laws are the greatest threat to your security and privacy in the real world. They allow anyone with an Internet connection to pierce the membrane separating the virtual world from the physical world.

This is the core of the problem and it might be a good time for us as a society to take a step back and reexamine these public records laws to see if they are really serving the public best interests.

When the public records laws were first passed, there was no Internet and everyone wasn't walking around with a mini supercomputer in their pocket. This is a classic case where advances in technology have outpaced advances in the legal process.

In simple terms, Public Records laws do serve the public interest:

Voter Records:	Prevent voter fraud
Land Records:	Settle land disputes
Arrest Records:	Transparency in law enforcement

But the massive advances in technology now makes these laws easy to abuse.

Voter and Land records:

If a person has moved in response to a traumatic event, such as stalking, and they purchase a home or vote, the public records of these activities could compromise their personal security. The public records will be acquired by public records search engines and then be published and accessible to anyone on the Internet. In the 1990's, if you wanted to get someone's address from Public Records, you would have to physically go to courthouse and manually search for them. Now these records are available anonymously with a few keystrokes and a mouse click. The common act of purchasing a home, or voting, should not put anyone's physical safety in jeopardy.

Arrest Records:

Arrest records were made public to provide transparency in the criminal justice system. They were never intended to be used to humiliate people by electronically publishing mugshots.

The widespread practice of news outlets posting the mugshots of people who have been arrested is nothing less than a form of cyberbullying. These people have not been convicted of any crimes so it is cruel to post photographs of them at a low point in their lives and allow people to anonymously post derogatory comments. The only reason anyone outside the immediate area is viewing these images is because the person is considered "Hot! Hot! Hot!" or has a crazy hair style.

The Public Records laws have not been updated at the same pace as advances in communication technology and do not address our current networked environment. They are simply man-made laws and can be changed.

In 1994, California passed the **Driver's Privacy Protection Act** in response to the stalking murder of actress Rebecca Schaeffer. Ms. Schaeffer was murdered after her stalker went to the DMV and pulled the young actress's home address from their public records. Had this incident taken place in 2012, her stalker would only have to use a public records search engine to get her home address.

We can let our lawmakers know that we value our privacy and can ask them to take a closer look at the existing public records laws and urge them take steps to change these laws and balance the public interest with providing better protection for ourselves and our families.

Removing Links from Search Engines:

If the various search results revealed other sensitive information about you, you will have to contact that website and request that the information be removed. If, for example, you had made a mistake and posted your phone number and/or email address and you wish these posts to be removed, you can locate the contact page of the website that is publishing your information.

After you contact the offending website, and request that the information be removed, you can send the offending link(s) to the various search engines and request that they remove the links from their query results. Remember, when you request that a link be removed, be sure to also request that the "**cached**" version be removed as well.

Google:

Google, true to their "Don't be Evil" creed, makes is easy for you to have links removed from their query results. Google provides an excellent tool for managing your information that is currently sitting on Google's systems.

This tool can be found at: **www.google.com/dashboard**

If you don't have a Google/Gmail account, create one using any of your other identities, and you can now control and monitor your personal information as well as have links removed from Google search results.

One of the more interesting features is the "**Me on the Web**" service where you can create alerts that are emailed to you whenever they show up in Google's databases. These alerts can be triggered on your name, phone number, or just about anything you want. If you are concerned about Google linking your virtual identity with your physical identity, you can "fuzz" the alerts. To "fuzz" your alerts, you can generate, say 20 different names in random order, but only one is your real name.

Then, on your local email client, create a message rule that will automatically delete any of these email alerts that do not contain your real information. Google will know you have 20 alerts set up, but not know which one is the real ID associated with the email address. It's not perfect, but it does provide a small degree of separation.

Bing/Yahoo:

Bing is Microsoft's search engine. If your information shows up in Bings's search results, go to:

www.bing.com/toolbox/webmaster/

There you will receive instructions on having links removed for their database.

Archive.org:

This is also known as the Internet way-back machine. This service takes snapshots of websites on the internet and archives them. If you have revealed personal information there is a chance this service has an archived copy. If you are able to find the offending link, then go to:

www.archive.org/about/exclude.php

AOL:

AOL uses Google for their search engine. Just follow the instructions for removing Google links.

With all of they search engines, be sure to submit the two links. The offending link and the cached link.

At this point in the game, you have removed most of the damaging disclosures of your privacy and have verified your social media profile privacy settings. Hopefully you also made a mental note to contact your lawmakers and encourage them to better protect your privacy.

Privacy in Social Media:

Social media sites, like Facebook, are a lot of fun to use. You can be reunited with old friends and classmates and they are a wonderful way to keep in touch with the people in your life. But, you need to be very careful with how you use social media to avoid potential problems in your future.

Unlike interstate data brokers, who acquire and publish public records, you personally have to take responsibility for what information you have disclosed to the Internet. After all, you signed up for the social media service. You provisioned your account with your personal information. You posted a picture of your kung pao chicken and wrote "YUM!".

Mark Zuckerberg, the founder of Facebook, said in an interview that privacy is dead and that if he were to create Facebook today, your profile would be public by default.

I would like to believe that privacy is not dead, but rather, privacy is in a coma - due to neglect.

I do agree with Mark's statement about making your profile public by default. This is not sucking up to Facebook, but rather a shared belief that if it was known up front that users could not hide their profile from public view, ever, they would be more careful about what information they would post in the first place.

People using social media sites like Facebook, LinkedIn, Google+, and Twitter, need to very aware of what information they are posting. There is no guarantee that it will remain private – so why post any potentially damaging information?

A good rule of thumb when posting anything on the Internet is this:

"**Do not post anything online that you would be uncomfortable with wearing on a t-shirt at the police station, when visiting your grandmother, or in front of the person you are talking about.**"

If you decide to use any social media site: Assume everything you post is public information.

Everything!

Google and Facebook allow you the ability to place your friends and family into separate groups. With these groups you can try to separate your different social activities.

You might post photos of you having a good time at the local bar but might not want your mother or coworkers to see you out drinking.

These groups are supposed to allow you to make certain posts visible to some groups and hidden from others. The problem with using groups in this manner is you can get lulled into a false sense of privacy when in reality you have no control over how these groups are managed by the social media sites.

Facebook has in the past reset user's privacy settings and made the user's profile public. Now your mother and coworkers can see you out at the bars and you might receive some negative comments on your offline activities. You can never fully trust any service provider to keep your activities hidden from prying eyes so the best policy is to always assume everything you do online is visible to everyone.

These groups can be thought of as mailing lists rather than secure compartments. If you assume that everything you post to any of the lists can be forwarded to any other group, you will be more careful about what information you post.

Try not to mix your social media activities. I use Facebook for my personal/social activities and use LinkedIn for my professional activities. Both of those services have minimal personal information and I am not relying on their ability or willingness to keep my activities compartmentalized and protected.

When provisioning your account in social media keep the personal information to the bare minimum. If you post your home address, phone number and clean email address, you have no idea who'll have access to this information in the future and there is no way you can unpublish it should there be a problem.

By updating your account with your home address and contact information, you open yourself up to potential problems in the real world.

Make a conscious effort to keep your physical and virtual worlds separate. Anyone close to you already has your contact information, so it is of little benefit to you to trust a social media site to safeguard your physical world information.

Most social media sites have a messaging capability so there is no real need to publish your email address. If you decide to provide an email address, be sure to use one of the dirty email addresses you had set up earlier.

When setting up a personal account on a social media site, do not use the default privacy settings. The default privacy settings are configured for the maximum benefit to the owners of the website and not for yours. If the service is free - then you and your information are the product.

After setting up your basic information on a social media site you will be urged to find your friends by uploading your email contact list. Please don't do it.

By uploading your contact list you are sending the personal information of everyone you have interacted with via email to unknown persons. It is convenient, but once you disclose the contact information of your friends, family, and coworkers, you cannot get it back. It is best to respect their privacy and provision your social media manually so you can skip the friend finding step – at least until after you have tightened up the privacy settings.

At this point you can begin modifying your social media account and privacy settings for your maximum benefit.

Facebook:

On Facebook, take a minute and review your account and verify that there is minimal personal information in your user profile.

Then go check out the "**Privacy settings**" and make sure that everything is set up to only allow people you know the ability to view your information. For Facebook, the default is "Public" meaning everything you do is visible to everyone. You will want to change this from "Public" to "Friends". By making this change then only people you "know", and Facebook, will have access to your profile information.

Even after you told Facebook to set your default privacy profile to "Friends", much of your information is still public.

On the "**How you Connect**" section, change who can look you up using an email address or phone number from "Everyone" to "Friends". This will limit the ability of over 400 million Facebook users from finding your profile by using your email address or your phone number.

You might want to restrict Facebook messaging to your friends list by changing the message setting from "Everyone" to "Friends". This can help reduce the amount of spam or any other kind of unwanted communication.

The next settings to visit are the **Profile and Tagging** sections.

Who can post on your Wall?

If you are concerned about any of your wacky friends posting something embarrassing onto your wall, then you can set the "Post to Wall" setting from "Friends" to "Only Me".

Who can see what others post on your profile?

You only want people you know to view your profile. I do understand that your profile can be made "Public" at any time, but it's a good idea to minimize access to your profile to people you have "friended" and not "Friends of Friends" and here's why.

According to the Surgeon General 20-% of people in the US currently suffer from some form of mental illness. According to the Department of Justice, the percentage of individuals suffering from mental illness and are also prone to violence, is estimated to be around 20%.*

If 20% of the population are suffering from a mental illness and 20% of those people are prone to violence, then the violent rate is about 4% of the population.

The average number of friends on Facebook is reported to be around 120 (although this number changes quite a bit)

**note: figures combined with substance abuse*

If you have the average number of Facebook friends and your current setting is set to "Friends Only", then this is the number of people who are prone to violence and have access to your Facebook page, status updates, photos and your personal information:

===> ….. <=== 4.8 people

If you change your privacy settings to allow "Friends of Friends" access, then this is the number of people who are prone to violence that you have viewing your private information:

....
....
....
....
....
.... <== 576 people

...and it only takes one to take a special interest in you to cause you problems in the real world. The lesson here is to be very careful who you "Friend" and allow access to your information on social media sites.

Review posts friends tag you in before they appear on your profile?

Disable all forms of tagging. Once you are tagged by someone you have no control over what happens with that information and who can view it. Recall that mobile app that provided a radar map of women in the area.

People have used this feature to embarrass and humiliate others on Facebook. Someone could take a picture of a dog's butt and tag it as you. If you have the chance to review any tags before they are published, you can completely avoid this possibility.

Who can see posts you've been tagged in on your profile?

Why stop at preview? You can use this setting to prevent any tagging of you from being published. It's a very good idea to disable this feature entirely.

Review tags friends add to your own posts on Facebook?

Clearly you want this feature turned on.

Who sees tag suggestions when photos that look like you are uploaded?

Facebook has facial recognition technology that will analyze photographs from other Facebook users and attempt to identify you.

If Facebook thinks they are able to identify you from any photos, they will suggest that you be tagged in the photo. This could be useful for finding other photos of you that have been posted without your knowledge.

The next block of Facebook privacy settings is **Apps and Websites.** Social media applications, or apps as they're called, are third party programs and games that can access your Facebook information.

There have been several published reports of application developers building 3rd party Facebook apps to hack Facebook and steal user account information. Facebook does not verify the integrity of 3rd party applications using their platform, so you need to be careful when clicking on any 3rd party apps or websites. The best bet is to elect to disable all Facebook apps in this section.

Apps you use:

Click on the "**Turn off all apps**" link. This is not a guarantee that Facebook will not share your information, but it does let them know that you wish to keep your account information from being shared with apps and other websites.

Instant Personalization:

This feature allows you to see information about your friends when you use other select websites that have partnered with Facebook. To do this, Facebook shares your public information with these partner websites:

Bing -	Social Search
Pandora -	Personalized Music
TripAdvisor -	Social Travel
Yelp -	Friends' Local Reviews
Rotten Tomatoes -	Friends' Movie Reviews
Clicker -	Personalized TV Recommendations
Scribd -	Social Reading
Docs -	Document Collaboration

I have the feature disabled. I love all of these sites, but I do not need for them to access my information nor care about what my friends are using. This is my personal choice. If you share this view, you can elect to disable this feature and click on the "confirm" button on the "Are you really really really sure?" window.

Public Search:

By default, your public account information is **not** submitted to search engines like Google and prevents anonymous Internet users from knowing you are on Facebook. If someone wants to find you on Facebook, they can join Facebook and try to look for you there.

Limit the Audience for Past Posts:

This feature allows you to limit the visibility of your past posts which may have been "Public" to "Friends". This is a very good feature to use – nice job Facebook!

This next section you have probably already used at some point in the past.

This is the **Blocked People and Apps**.

Any person or application that you find annoying can be easily blocked. Once blocked, they will not be able to have any access to you or your information.

I find this feature useful in blocking automated posts by applications. If you block Farmville, for example, you will see fewer posts from friends telling you that they have just fed their chickens.

Once you have your Privacy controls in place, you can revisit your account setting and put these changes in context.

Account Settings:

General:

The General account setting page will display the basic information you had provided when you created your Facebook account. The important section here is "linked accounts".

Facebook allows you the ability to link your Facebook account to your other online accounts such as Google, Yahoo, and Myspace to name a few. I don't link my accounts because I want each of my accounts to be completely separate from each other. If one of those accounts gets hacked, my other accounts are still safe. If you have linked accounts, then there is a chance that a compromise of one account will leak over and compromise your other accounts.

Security:

Under the security section of your account settings, the important option on this page is the **Secure Browsing** link. Edit this setting and select the "**Browse Facebook on a secure connection (https) when possible**".

Note this says *"when possible"* and is, therefore, not a guarantee. By selecting this option, you are telling Facebook to protect your entire Facebook session from eavesdropping.

As we've seen in the "Safe Computing" section, if you are browsing your Facebook account at a local cafe, anyone with a wireless connection and some hacker software can monitor your activities. If your session is protected by a secure connection, your activities are better protected from snooping.

Notifications Settings:

The notification section allows you to control how you are notified when someone interacts with your Facebook account. You can send your notifications to an email address or by text message to your cellphone.

This feature is very useful because you will be warned when someone does something that could be potentially embarrassing to you on your Facebook account.

The important setting to use to help maintain your Facebook page and prevent embarrassment, is to make sure you are notified when someone posts something onto your wall or tries to tag you in a post. These settings are located in the **Facebook** link.

If you post photos, you will want to be notified whenever someone either "tags" you, or posts a comment on one of your photos.

Facebook has all of these types of notifications turned on by default and this is a very good thing. If someone does anything that you might consider inappropriate or embarrassing, you can immediately go on to Facebook and delete, or report, any offensive activities.

The next important section is related to your notification settings. The **Mobile settings** page will allow you to be notified by text message instead of email when someone interacts with your Facebook account.

This is extremely useful in managing your Facebook account. You will be notified instantly when something you might not like is posted to your wall or when someone tries to tag you in a note or an unflattering photograph. By sending you a text message, you can respond quickly and remove the activity from your account.

The next section is very important. The **Facebook ad** section allows you some control over ads shown by third parties. This page clearly states "Facebook does not give third party applications or ad networks the right to use your name or picture in ads. If we allow this in the future, the setting you choose will determine how your information is used."- *Well, there goes my "Hemorrhoid cream" lawsuit.*

If you are uncomfortable with the possibility that Facebook will allow your photographs to be used in advertising by third parties, you can watermark the photos you wish to protect.

This is not perfect, as there are a large number watermark removal tools available on the Internet, but it will at least be known that you had made an attempt to protect your photographs.

To prevent Facebook, and their 3rd party affiliates, from using your personal photos in advertising you can "opt-out" by setting the option from "**Only my friends**" to **"No One"**.

The other setting to consider on this page is the "**Ads and friends**" section. If you "like" a sushi joint on Facebook, ads for the restaurant will inform your friends that you "like" it and may display your profile picture. If you are uncomfortable with this possibility, you can "opt-out" and change the "**Pair my social actions with ads**" setting from **"Only my friends"** to "**No One**".

Now that your account and privacy setting are under control, you can then return to editing the information of your account profile. This reason we tightened up our account and privacy settings is to prevent the accidental disclosure of your information before your account has been "secured".

When you click on your name on your Facebook page, you are given the opportunity to edit your personal profile.

Before adding any information to your profile, consider whether your friends really need to know this information. It is very likely that all of your close friends already know where you work or where you are going to school, so there really is no point in posting this information.

The same is true with posting your contact information. Facebook offers a "private" messaging capability, so if any of your virtual friends needs to get in touch, they have a way to send you a message.

If your account gets hacked, then your information is disclosed to people you do not know. Always assume your account will get hacked. This is not to say that it would, but if you knew your account would be hacked tomorrow, then what would you want to do today to protect yourself.

If you are already using Facebook, then consider removing all of the information that might affect you in the real world. Your workplace information will give anyone your physical location during the day. Your address will let someone know where you sleep at night. Your contact information will provide way to stalk and harass you.

With this in mind, it's a good time to purge your account of any information you would not be comfortable disclosing face-to-face with a complete stranger. Anyone close to you in the real world already has this information so there is little benefit to you to have this information available online.

When editing your profile, there are two sections that you should be most concerned with. One is "**Friends and Family**" and the other is "**Contact Information.**"

Friends and Family:

This section allows you to control the visibility of your friends and family. The default for the setting is "**Public**", and is viewable to every Facebook user.

There's no benefit to you to have this information visible. Your friends and family list can be used against you at some point in the future and could encourage you to accept friend requests from people impersonating people from your past. If you are in a relationship and it starts to go south, your former partner can try to get to you by communicating with or harassing your friends and family. I know who my mom and children are, so there is no need for me to make this information public.

Facebook currently does not verify the identity of anyone setting up an account. Anyone can set up an account on Facebook using a false identity – all they need is a valid email address.

If someone you wanted to avoid wants to get to you, they can look up your friends and grab a profile picture of one of them. Then re-size and make a few changes to the photo and upload the photo to a fake account they have set up using a similar name of one of your friends and then contact you. You would likely think your real friend had mistakenly defriended you and could accept the request from the imposter.

Another tactic would be for someone to gather information about you from your friends list. If they see a large number of friends sharing a common theme – like they all went to the same high school – then this person could use a service like Classmates.com and get the names and possibly photos of your high school classmates using a fake identity.

With this list of your classmates, the person can then create an account impersonating someone from your high school class. You will see their picture and gladly accept the friend request. Now your information and Facebook activities can be monitored by your jealous ex. You can change the visibility of your friends and family by changing the privacy setting from "**Public**" to "**Only Me**".

Under the "**Contact Information**" page, the settings are set to "**Friends**" by default. Since all of your friends and family already have a way to get in touch with you, and Facebook provides a messaging feature, you can tighten up your privacy settings and change all of these from "**Friends**" to "**Only Me**".

Spring Cleaning:

At this point, you can take a look at your wall and think about tidying things up a bit. I only keep about a month's worth of status updates on my wall at any given time. I have a strict, "post-one/delete-one" policy and it helps me keep track of all of my information. The same is true with my private messages. Once the conversation is over, I delete the message thread and I usually only keep photos up for a few weeks.

I have the original photographs so I do not need to have Facebook store my personal photographs and am uncomfortable with the possibility that these photos could be used in advertising cat food at some point in the future.

Facebook makes it very easy to post status updates, and share information. To post a status update, all you have to do is type in a brief description of the event that you just felt compelled to share with all of your friends, and then press the enter key. It's posted!

Facebook makes it more difficult to remove information from your page. If you decided to delete that status update that you had just posted a few seconds ago, you would have to click on the status, then scroll down and select "Delete", then confirm that wanted to delete your status and not share the fact that you have just watched a hilarious Family Guy episode with your friends.

That is a 3-to-1 ratio. Deleting information from Facebook takes 3 times the effort than sharing information. You might think it would be the opposite – but, there is a reason for this. Facebook and other social media sites want as much of your information as possible.

Don't play their game; purge your Facebook account on regular basis. There is no need for your Facebook account to contain years and years of pictures of your food and your quirky, hilarious, status updates.

There is little benefit for you to keep more than a few months worth of status updates alive and it'll be much more time consuming when you decide trim your Facebook account when you have several years of status updates.

If you only keep your Facebook page limited to a single page – it's much easier to maintain and you know exactly what is currently posted and sitting on Facebook's servers. An additional benefit is you will not have to deal with the beloved Facebook Timeline format.

Friending:

Anyone you don't know in the physical world should not be a friend on Facebook or other personal social media websites. Try to keep your personal friends on Facebook and your business contacts on LinkedIn and every so often, consider purging your friends list and only keep those who you really know.

If you receive a friend request on Facebook, you might be tempted to accept the request if you see that you have some mutual friends with this person - but a friend of a friend is really a complete stranger.

There is a common practice on social media sites that is known as "Facebook Grooming". Grooming occurs when someone is contacted on a social media site by an individual that has an objective, or ulterior motive, in mind. This objective can range from the flattering, such as wanting a date, to malicious involving financial scams and sexual predation.

In 2011, a gang of men in England groomed as many as 139 young girls on social media sites. They would take their time, earn the trust of these young women, and eventually arrange to meet them in the real world where they were given alcohol and then assaulted.

When someone is groomed on social media sites, they are first contacted by someone they do not directly know, but might be friends-of-a-friend and so, accept the request. After the groomer contacts their target, the next phase is to attempt to gain their trust.

If you had a received a message or friend request from someone that was crude or offensive, you would likely ignore it and put a block on the sender to prevent them from contacting you in the future. But a groomer is slick and they will go though your profile in an attempt to learn all they can about you to find anything they can use to help tailor their pitch to you.

If you love the music group Rammstein – they might post the *Haifisch* music video on your wall. If they learn that you are politically conservative, they can post Ayn Rand quotes and make comments about Rush Limbaugh's latest rant. The groomer will share your beliefs, celebrate your victories and console you when you are down.

During this process of gaining your trust, the groomer will look for a vulnerability that they can then exploit. It can be something a simple as offering words of comfort if you post that you are feeling tired or are going through a personal struggle or giving you a heads-up for a job opportunity if they know that you are unemployed.

Their objective here is to fulfill a need that they know you have.

In the hacker world, this activity is known as Social Engineering. A groomer will use the information you have posted to engineer an online relationship with you in an attempt to gain your trust and achieve their hidden objective.

After weeks of chatting and exchanging comments online, you might think you are real friends with the groomer and can now be lured into meeting in the real world. This can be done overtly - "Hey, let's get coffee.." - or covertly, as in arranging to bump into you when you post that you will be at a certain event. This is where you have to be careful.

When you meet someone traditionally in the real world, you get a feel for who this person is and can take your time getting to know them before you would consider them to be a friend.

When you meet a person online, the only information you have about this person is the information that they have provided you. Since all of your communication is online, you only get a partial picture of who they are and cannot pick up on any of those subtle, non-verbal cues that could indicate there is a problem with this person that you might have sensed when talking with them face-to-face.

As the online chatting continues, your brain fills in the blanks and you can begin to feel that you are actually real-world friends with someone you have never met.

They are not real friends, they are only acquaintances at best. You may exchange emails or comment on each other's posts but your relationship with these people is all in your mind.

When you meet someone in the physical world that you have been chatting with online, it might be hard to remember that you really do not know this person and you might be tempted to let your guard down.

You have to force yourself to remember that you have to start the whole relationship process over again before you can begin to trust someone you have met online.

A friend-of-a-friend is a total stranger and should be treated as such until they have earned your trust, over time, in the real world.

Employment:

Social media and the Employment issue is a literal minefield so be very aware of what you share online. Anything you post does have the potential to negatively impact your professional life as will the people you are associated with. The old "birds of a feather" line of thinking can diminish your ability to find a job.

In any employment situation, chances are good that you have already been low-level stalked. Potential employers will check you out online. They will look at Facebook, LinkedIn, and search for your name in news articles to see if you have ever been arrested.

They may even kick it up a notch and use an online public records search. If you have been convicted of a crime, it is reasonable for an employer know this information – either through self disclosure or through a public records search. It is always the best policy to come clean and explain to a prospective employer what has happened, what you have learned from the experience and how you've bettered yourself. If the employer finds out any other way – your chances of a job go to zero.

Another problem with employers accessing social media sites is there may not be any incriminating or embarrassing information on your Facebook page. But, if your employer has access to your "friends" list, you might have a friend that your employer knows who beat up his kid or backed over her cat and be blackballed because of that.

The best policy for using social media sites is to minimize the amount of personal information residing in your account and be very aware of what information you are sharing. That way, if you are a final candidate for a job, and the nice HR woman asks you to log into your Facebook account while they watch, you will have less to worry about.

If I was ever requested to show my Facebook, or any other account, I would, stand up and smile and politely say, "No, thank-you" and leave. End of interview. I really hope this practice stops soon.

Now that your Facebook presence is cleaned up, you can apply these same privacy principals to any of your other social media accounts like Google+, LinkedIn, Twitter and Myspace.

Relationships and Dating:

Internet dating is hilarious. I've done it a few times. It happens. Don't judge.. and I found it to be an interesting way to meet people outside of my normal social circles. It's much better than hanging around some bar or going to singles events and I have met some very nice people this way.

The best part of meeting people on-line is hearing their dating stories. For some reason I just love hearing bad date stories. Not the ones that are horrible and scary and involve the police, but the ones that are just funny. After talking with my female friends and other women, there appears to be a lot of subterfuge going on in the on-line dating scene so don't be too surprised if any of this ever happens to you.

People lie about their availability. Several of my female friends have reported their date's relationship status slipped from "Divorced", to "Separated" and then, finally to "...still living with her until we figure out what to do with the house and the cats".

People will lie about their income. They may drive up in a BMW, but they could park that BMW in a low income apartment complex. The money issue appears to be more important to men than to women – so why do some people lie about it?

And the biggest lie....

Men lie about their height on-line. I find this very funny and will probably take some heat for mentioning the height issue. It's not as though you would not notice that your date is looking at your chin when you wear high-heels. Some men use little height enhancing lifts but the only shoe inserts that might be acceptable to women would be solid gold bars; at least then she would have a choice between dating a rich liar or fleeing from someone who's feet are effectively bolted to the floor.

If you find yourself single and decide to date, in either the real world or online, you can take a number of precautions now that will help minimize future problems.

Online Dating:

When setting up your on-line dating profile, "fuzz" your information. By fuzzing, I mean to modify your information a little bit. Instead of placing your town, consider placing a few towns over. Instead of posting your real age, add or subtract a few years (but only a few).

Add or subtract an inch or two to or from your height and simply state you have kids, but offer no clues as to how many. This will help prevent anyone from being able to search for you based on your known unique characteristics – like a jealous ex.

If you decide to post photos, make them hidden until you have decided to contact someone and only then allow them to be viewed. On the dating website, Plenty-of-Fish (www.plentyoffish.com), they offer that option and joining is free.

Any photos that you send, make sure they are not geotagged and that they are stripped of any revealing information – such as the file name should not be "cindy2010.jpg" nor contain any other information (for example a photo of your license plate, your house number, or some notable, visible, landmark near your home). Many websites will strip out this information when you upload your photos, but do it yourself to be certain.

On Windows, you can strip photos of any meta-data, by right clicking the photo. Then clicking "Properties", then clicking on "Details" and then the link to "Remove Properties and Personal Information". For the MAC, the process is a bit more involved but here is a simple trick.

Open an image in Preview, and then save it as a PNG, then open up that image and save it back to a JPEG. The meta-data has been stripped from the file and you can safely send the image without revealing any location information – but be sure to verify the data has been stripped out.

I would consider obtaining a tool to strip all of your photos of their meta-data. There many free, publicly available tools that can do this on both the Windows and Mac platforms. Search for "photo meta-data removal" using your favorite search engine.

After your profile is set up and you begin getting swamped with emails, be very careful not to reveal too much of your location identity to anyone before you get to know them. This can include where you live, work and where you like to go out on Friday nights. A friend of mine used to enjoy Latin dancing on Wednesday nights and she made the mistake of telling this to someone she had just met online. The very next Wednesday night, guess who shows up uninvited and gets angry that she's dancing with other guys?

To avoid the arranged "bump in", try to keep your physical location and social schedule private, until you get to know them a little better.

When you receive an email from a prospective suitor online, do not reply from your email account. Instead, log into the on-line dating site and send your reply from there (or not, if there's a shirtless shot of them sitting on a Harley holding a puppy).

When you reply from the email account on your computer, you would have revealed your email address and your IP address. Your IP address could then be mapped to a rough estimate of your physical location. If you did reply from your email, then hopefully you used the throwaway email address you provided when setting up your account.

Real World Dating:

When you meet someone in the real world, be aware of what personal information you disclose and avoid offering your phone number. Instead, offer them one of those throw-away email addresses you have previously set up. This is to help prevent them from getting enough information to perform a free public records search that would reveal your full identity.

If you receive an email from this new person – feel free to search on the name and email address fields. I have a friend who did this with an email he received from a woman he met online. The email revealed her full name and when searched, a news article popped up that reported she had been arrested for domestic violence against her husband and son the previous year. I guess it didn't matter because he still dated her – briefly.

When you receive any email, from either the real world or an on-line dating site, be careful clicking on any links contained in the email. These links could be phishing attempts to obtain your private log in information. If you click on a link and you are prompted to log in, do not enter your log in information. If the link is supposed to be from the dating website, you can open up a web browser and go directly to that site to view the message. Any email that contains a link that requires you to log in, should be considered very suspicious and if the email contains an attachment, be sure to scan it first with your security software. Email attachments can contain keystroke loggers and spy software, so it's important to run every attachment through your security software before viewing them.

The Dreaded Phone Call:

After a time of e-mailing back and forth, you and your date will want to take the relationship to a new level:

The dreaded phone call.

Many people hate this part and a useful trick at this phase is to pretend you're talking with an old friend you haven't heard from in a while. You basically have the same amount of information at that time, right?

Preceding the Dreaded Phone Call, you have talked about exchanging phone numbers. At this point you have a choice. Do you want to disclose your phone number?

You can opt to call them - but, before doing so, be sure to block your outgoing Caller-ID. You want to protect your phone number because it is a direct link to you in the real world but be aware, CallerID blocking is not perfect.

Reconsider giving out your personal phone number to people you do not know. The phone number can be called repeatedly, and at all hours of the night, posted on Craigslist, or a bathroom wall and so you need to protect your phone number.

Texting:

If your new friend gives you her or his cellphone number, resist the urge to send a text message.

As we've learned earlier, even when Caller-ID is blocked, anytime you send a text message from your cellphone, your phone number is displayed.

There is currently no way to disable this, so avoid sending a text message to someone you do not wish to have your phone number.

If you feel a strong need to text someone, you can do it through the Internet, or send it from one of your "Dirty" email addresses.

AT&T:	Send an email from your "Dirty" email address to: **number@txt.att.net**
Verizon:	Send an email from your "Dirty" email address to: **number@vtext.com**

There are also a number of websites on the Internet that will allow you to send semi-anonymous text messages.

Like with protecting your "Clean" email address, only communicate by voice using a throw-away phone number.

Secure Phone:

You can obtain a throw away phone number easily. The free option is to get an account on Google Voice. Google Voice offers you an unlisted phone number attached to your Google account that will be forwarded to any number you want and it's free.

Some of you might have a problem with Google knowing about your calls or your real phone number. If this is the case you can go into Secret Agent mode and visit Walmart, or any other place and purchase a pay-per-use phone for cash.

The number of your pay-per-use phone can be disclosed to whomever you want because there is no way for a civilian to track that phone back to you in the real world.

If you want to go into Super Stealth mode, you can purchase a used pay-as-you-go phone online and pay in cash while employing your new privacy protection plan.

Consider your real phone number your "Clean" phone and the throwaway number your "Dirty" phone. This is the phone number you use to talk to people you do not yet fully trust. You can keep the conversations short and not chew up your minutes while you get an auditory feel for who you are talking with. This is your secured communications channel and should be used for all voice communication with people you have just met..

If your potential date ever calls you on a number you did not disclose - it is *not* flattering - it is creepy and you are being stalked on some level. This behavior should raise a huge red flag.

Should there be a problem and someone starts to harass you on your dirty phone, you can simply toss that phone away and get a new number. End of problem. If you are using Google voice, you can pay a $10 fee and get a new number.

The Meet and Greet:

After you've talked for a while (and no texts unless from your throwaway pay-per-use phone or through the Internet), you will want to meet your new friend in person and see if they will pass the autonomic nervous system test.

Your autonomic nervous system is your body's gift to you that helps keep you safe in the real world. It's the source of that uneasy feeling you get in the pit of your stomach. That feeling is millions of years of evolutionary engineering at work protecting you from an unpleasant experience.

If your date shows up wearing clown shoes and has sparklers in their hair, it might just trigger that uneasy feeling... as might any of the cast members of Jersey Shore. If you get that feeling, even if you cannot explain it or it makes no logical sense, do not try to rationalize or ignore it.

Your body is sounding the alarm for a reason and is trying to protect you. If you get that sinking feeling, do not hesitate to make up an excuse and leave – just be sure you are not followed out. Dogs are excellent at detecting this unconscious danger, so you might consider bringing yours along....but leave the cat at home.

Before your meet and greet, take your cellphone and set a timer – or you can use the Google Calendar service to send you a text message at a predetermined time.

If the date is not going well, or your body starts trying wave you off of this person, then it would be a good break point and simply state "It's my Mom, I have to go help... blah blah blah" and leave. You can also have a friend call or send you a text at a preset time – but I find that Google and countdown timers are more reliable. If it's not going well and you elect to "opt-out", your date has no real information about you and so – Poof! They're gone.

For your physical security, agree to meet in a very public place that you do not frequent outside of your town. This is to help prevent them trying to seek you out in the future and arrange to "bump" into you.

Try get there a little early and select a seat in a conspicuous place and make a mental note of the exits and the proximity to other patrons.

When your date arrives, you can then begin what is hopefully a pleasant journey. Try not to drink alcohol before you get a better feel for this person – just meet for coffee. The purpose of this date is to see of there is any chemistry and also to see if they set off any unconscious alarms.

Sunny Skies:

As the relationship progresses and they begin to earn your trust, you will feel comfortable revealing more of your personal information. But try not to reveal too much until you are sure you fully trust your new found friend.

If your new friend questions you about some of your precautions, you can simply state you are careful because you have had some problems in the past – if they don't respect that and pressure you– that could be a red flag.

So take your time, enjoy and not rush the process.

And, by the way, congratulations on your new relationship!

Stormy Skies:

At some point every relationship can get a little weird. This section is not about dispensing relationship advice – you can watch Dr. Phil for that - but there are a few things to watch out for to better protect yourself.

There is really only one sign that your relationship is in trouble:

You feel your relationship is in trouble.

I believe that everyone is entitled to their own personal privacy and I will not recommend that anyone go creeping though their partner's stuff in the hope of catching them at something. It is a futile effort. If you think your partner is cheating on you or suspect the relationship is in trouble, have a sit down heart-to-heart with them when you both have each other's full attention.

But the reality is this person has all of your personal information so if you suspect things are not going well, you can take a few steps to protect your privacy.

Step 1:

Verify your computer hasn't been compromised. When someone becomes suspicious, they may install software on your system to watch everything you do. Some of the spy software will enable the camera/webcam and they could be watching you without your knowledge or consent. To help prevent this, repeat the steps in the "**Securing your Laptop / Computer"** section.

Step 2:

If you find your system has been tampered with or suspect your partner knows your passwords, then reset all of the passwords for every device and service you use.

Computer: Prevent access to your emails, and installing spy software

Cellphone: Prevent access to your texts, call history etc.

Banking: Prevent stealing money or watching your account activities.

Credit Cards: Prevent watching your spending.

Social Media: Prevent viewing your messages or posting things as you.

Shopping: Prevent from viewing purchase history and or make embarrassing purchases on your behalf.

Any service you use that has a password, change it.

Step 3:

Cyberstalk yourself. See if any of your personal information has been posted on Craigslist or any other sites. Repeat the steps found in "**Online Privacy Profile**" section of this book.

Step 4:

Search for yourself on any shared computer. If you have a "house" computer, search the entire system for references to you. (*I have a friend who was getting a little uneasy in her relationship. One day, she was poking through the house computer and she discovered a chat script where her husband had been online soliciting sex - posing as her.*)

Step 5:

Search for yourself on on-line dating sites. Just enter your stats and see if your photo or any profile resembling you, pops up. If you see your information on an on-line or adult dating site, contact them immediately and have the profile removed.

Step 6:

Be aware of anything unusual. Be on the alert for unusual packages, or USB flash drives or if your computer is acting strange. Be on the alert for unusual phone calls, or text messages from unknown numbers. If you find or receive a USB flash drive, or camera card. Do not place it in an unsecured computer. Be sure to scan the media first with your security software.

We've Lost Cabin Pressure:

When an intimate relationship, or even a friendship, ends it is a very stressful event for all parties involved. If you were the one who was informed that the relationship is over, as painful as it is, just accept this fact and move on. Nothing good will from trying to win them back.

If you are the one who ended the relationship, be very aware of any future threats. By ending the relationship respectfully and with kindness, you improve your chances that there will be not any problems in the future.

However, if you start posting derogatory remarks of your Ex on social media sites, or worse, post photos of you and your new friend, it is neither kind, nor respectful to your past relationship and it could also trigger stalking behavior.

Some people, for whatever the reason, even when you are gentle in ending the relationship, will become very angry and could start bullying or stalking you in both the real and virtual world.

If it comes to your attention that someone is posting derogatory statements about you on social media sites like Facebook - report it. Facebook, is very responsive to requests to remove offending information. I have used it a few times and Facebook's response could be measured in seconds.

Any communication that you consider harassing or threatening, should be acted upon immediately. Warn your friends and family that you think you are having a problem with this person and ask them to be on the alert for any communication from them.

Instruct them to not provide any information about you to anyone at this time and to notify you of any communication with your Ex. If they receive any electronic communication, ask them to provide you with copies of the messages.

Whenever you receive an electronic message that you would consider to be threatening or harassing, you can do several things.

1) Reply to the email, including the full name and contact information of the sender, if available, and clearly state that you consider the communication harassing and threatening.

2) Clearly state that you do not wish to be contacted again

3) Send the email and carbon-copy the police, campus police and the ISP of the sender. If the message was sent from gmail.com account - notify Google. If from a yahoo.com account - notify Yahoo. To learn where to report harassing and threatening emails search for "report threats" on the service provider's home page.

4) Preserve a copy of all communications with this individual.

5) If it happens again in any form or situation escalates, go to the police and obtain a restraining order.

Informing the police early will help in two ways. It will communicate to your Ex that you are serious about protecting yourself and your family.

In the event that the situation gets completely out of control and you or your family is threatened, it will give the police a place to start. Recall that story about "Jeffrey", the stalker – he took the time and had assembled a little kit.

Electronic Tracking:

There have been many cases where a jealous Ex will plant a GPS device or a cellphone on a vehicle to track their victim. GPS trackers are small, inconspicuous, devices that can be purchased on eBay/Amazon and will report your position until the battery runs out.

If you are concerned about your vehicle being tracked, bring it to a trusted mechanic or friend and have them inspect your car for anything suspicious.

You can also contact your cellphone carrier, either through the phone or on their website, and make sure your phone is not currently being tracked using the GPS location feature. While you are at it, verify the number of phones that are on the account. Ask them to remove any secret phones that you were not aware of.

If you find any suspicious devices – go to the police immediately and report it.

Sometimes a breakup can get completely out of control so if you are concerned, it might be a good idea to contact your local woman's support group and get some advice. They have a lot of experience dealing with these types of issues and will be able to point you in the right direction while supporting you at this time.

Cyberstalking/Cyberbullying:

Cyberstalking and Cyberbullying are essentially the same thing and describe an activity that can be very damaging and scar the victim. There are reported statistics that range from 30% to 80% of people will be harassed electronically in their lifetime. The reason is that harassing someone electronically is very easy to do and it is essentially risk-free.

Being obnoxious to another person face-to-face in the real world has risks. The Internet and cellphones allow someone to make threats and harass people anonymously without the risk of getting their asses kicked in the real world.

A good general rule for anyone posting anything on the Internet is this: "Never say electronically what you would be too afraid to say to someone's face".

It's cowardly – simple as that.

Cyberstalking can include:

- Sending harassing e-mails, instant messages and text messages and images

- "Doxing" - a hacker term for invading a person's privacy and exposing all of their personal information on the Internet for the world to see. Think Julian Assange and WikiLeaks.

- Impersonating a person online which is especially serious. There has been cases where people have been sexually assaulted because someone posted a fake "Rape Fantasy" ad on Craigslist. In 2012, a man in Oregon posted ads on Craigslist while impersonating his ex-girlfriend.

- Inciting violence online against you or your family

If you are aware of any of this behavior to you or your family, you have to act immediately. The first step is to locate the offending posts, emails, text messages and preserve them.

The next step is to contact any and all websites that are hosting these offending articles and messages and have them take the offending information down – immediately.

Facebook and other social media sites are very responsive to reports of abuse. Then contact the search engines and have them remove any links to the offending content as well as the cached copy.

If the offending communication is in email form, follow the steps for dealing with email threats covered earlier.

If the communication form is a call or a text/SMS message, go online and attempt a reverse number look up.

You will not see the name of the sender, but you will learn which carrier owns the phone number that the message was sent from. Call up that carrier and report the threat.

Next, contact your carrier and report the incident and request a block be placed on the sending phone number.

Blocked Call Hacker Trick:

Most likely any harassing phone calls will have the Caller ID blocked. You can always just dump the call to voice-mail and then delete it without listening to it. Or, you can use a sneaky hacker trick and find out who's been calling you with caller ID blocked without going to the police and getting a search warrant. Pretend you're a celebrity and are getting these annoying calls and get yourself another cellphone and sign up for a 1-800 number. It's fast easy and cheap(ish). You can sign up for a free trial and only use it for a little while.

If you are a truly a celebrity, then you might want to consider using this technique all of the time. Configure "call forwarding" on the old cellphone, the one that is receiving the blocked calls, to your new 1-800 number. Then forward your 1-800 number to your new cellphone number. The next time you get a call with caller ID blocked, the real number will show up on the new cellphone. You can take that number to the police and place a block on it with your cellphone carrier. The original cellphone number is your "dirty" number and the new cellphone number is your "clean" number – and should be guarded with care.

If you do not wish to set this up yourself, you can subscribe to TrapCall.com. Trapcall.com offers a service where you can unmask blocked CallerID on your cellphone. When you receive a call that has the CallerID blocked, you simply reject the call and the call is automatically forwarded to the TrapCall service for unmasking and then back to your phone with the unblocked number. No more blocked calls!

If you are concerned for your safety, or the safety of a family member – report the harassment to your local police department.

If you suspect a friend or someone in your family is cyberbullying, confront them about it. There is no excuse for this behavior and there should be no tolerance – ever.

Cyberstalking/Bullying is rampant, so it is best for you to be aware of this pervasive activity to better protect you and your family from its impact. If you see it – act now.

Protecting Your Children:

There are currently laws on the books that protect the privacy of children under 13. The Children's Online Privacy Protection Act (COPPA) gives parents some control over what information websites can collect from their children's online activities.

What is interesting is what happens to that data when your child achieves the threshold age of 13? Is all of that previously protected information now fair game? I do think the law is a great start and it does have teeth. There have been several successful cases prosecuted for violating this act and the fines have been substantial.

As adults, we live in a privacy protection vacuum where important people, like Judges, have to make a conscious effort to remove their personal information from the systems of online information brokers. Even Judges have no power to remove any of the public records that have been exported and are now sitting on systems that are outside the jurisdiction of the United States government.

If all of our personal information is unprotected sitting on servers around the globe, how can we protect our children when we cannot fully protect ourselves?

As a parent, the best thing you can do to protect your children is to first be aware of the risks involved when children go online and address it honestly: It can happen to your family. I know it is a horrible thought but it does happen. An excellent starting point for protecting your children in the virtual and physical world can be found at the Center for Missing and Exploited Children at

www.missingkids.com

The next thing is to be sure to have an ongoing discussion about the privacy and security issues you have learned. I say ongoing, because since the threat is invisible, it is easy to ignore. By having an ongoing dialogue with your children, you can better educate and protect them.... and yourself.

The third step is to take steps to protect your own privacy. If anyone wants to get to your kids, they will have to find them and the easiest way to find them is to find their parents. Public records searches make this trivial to do.

Hopefully, by this point, you are more aware of your privacy and if you haven't set your laptop on fire or smashed your cellphone with a hammer, you can apply this new awareness to protecting the privacy and safety of your children.

Keystroke Logger:

You can start protecting the privacy of your child by invading their privacy and installing a keystroke logger onto their computer. Be sure to lock the children out of any other computers in the house and do not give them a smartphone or other Internet capable device thus forcing them to use the system with the installed key-logger. Whether you tell them that you are watching their online activities is up to you.

By installing a key-logger, the computer activities of anyone, including you, will be recorded and stored and there will be no secret Facebook, or MySpace, accounts accessed from the family computer.

Many parents claim that their children do not have Facebook accounts. How can they be sure? Your minor child could create a Facebook account and block you from seeing it.

You can also apply the "**Personal Privacy Profile**" exercise outlined earlier, only look for your children. If you find an account on a social media site – then you can decide what you want to do. If you want the account removed, you can notify the service provider and request that the account be removed from their systems – but be sure to follow though and have any links removed from the search engines as well.

Social media sites, like Facebook and MySpace, currently ban children under 13, but could enforce an "adults only" account registration policy by simply asking for a valid credit card. Not to charge, but as some proof that the account creator is a legal adult.

They could generate a cryptographic signature of that credit card information, like the one-way SHA-2 hash function, and prevent that same card from be reused while not retaining any of the credit card information. The SHA-2 hash functions are the cryptographic algorithms used in the U.S. Government for the protection of sensitive information and will allow a service to verify information without having to store the information in the clear.

The reason these social media sites don't "allow" anyone under 13 is the Children's Online Privacy Protection Act (COPPA). This act is enforced and there have been significant penalties for violations so the safe thing for any social media site to do is to not "allow" children under 13.

If you find your child has a stealth social media account, they will be highly motivated to remove it. To have your child's account removed, you will have to contact the site operators and provide proof of your identity and your child's account information.

Photographs of your Children:

According to the Center for Missing and Exploited children 1 in 7 children who are regular Internet users will receive a sexual solicitation on-line and 1 in 25 will receive a request to meet in real life.

I saw a demonstration of this – Live.

Years ago I gave a talk in Connecticut, and after my presentation, a member of law enforcement set up a computer and displayed the screen to a large projector in the auditorium. The officer then logged into an Internet chat room with a screen name of something like "boredGurl12" and posted "hey.."

And the projection screen exploded. I remember being shocked by the number of pop-up chat requests that filled the screen. The officer sent a few replies and then it got very, very creepy..

"where r U @?"

"$U like older guy$?"

So it happens and there is a remote chance that your child could be lured away by someone they have met online. That is why you have to take some precautions beforehand.

Always have a current photograph of your children and instruct your child to tell you whenever anyone takes their picture.

Not in a scary way, but just casually. Child pornography is rampant. When working with law enforcement, I had learned that each investigator was currently working on 5-10 active cases. Therefore, you will want to be very aware of anyone taking a special interest in photographing your child.

Secret Code Word:

Establish a security protocol with your children and make it simple and easy to understand. That way, if your child has "run away" and you receive any form of monitored communication with your child, you can establish the fact that your child had been abducted and has not run away.

This happens in the sex traffic trade. Young people, both male and female, get lured away by someone and to prevent any investigation, their captors will allow them brief, monitored, communication with their parents. If this is the case, a security code will be very helpful.

Here's an example:

Mom: "You sound tired, are you?"
(Are you OK or in physical danger?)

Child: "I have an **earache**...but I'm OK. "
(Help! I've been kidnapped!!)

Mom: "Is your **asthma** bothering you?"
(Are you OK or in physical danger?)

Child: "I **coughed** a lot today, but I'm OK"
(Help! I've been kidnapped!!)

If the exchange is monitored, your child might tell you that they've run away and they are happier where they are now, but by using your secret code, the abductors will not know their prisoner has revealed the fact that they are being held against their will.

You can practice using this system in everyday situations to secretly communicate with your child without the risk of offending anyone who might overhear the conversation.

Mom: "Are you having fun at Grampa's house?"

Child: "Yeah, it's great! Did **Fluffy come home** yet?"
(Help! We're having turnips for dinner! Come get me!)

If your child is ever missing, give the police the child's computer and inform them of the key-logger. This will allow the police access to all of the activity on that computer and could provide access to any hidden accounts. Accessing all of your child's online accounts will allow the police to be able to review all of their communications and this information could be critical in an investigation.

Nothing Good Happens After Midnight:

Many of the wireless routers that you use to connect to the Internet will allow you to "**Shut Off**" the Internet at certain times. This is known as Service Filtering or Access Restrictions.

You can configure your wireless router to only allow Internet access to specific computers at certain times of day.

Go online and search for the make and model of your wireless router. This information will be located on either the front, or back panels of your wireless router. Look for the Access Restriction, or Filter sections of the user manuals.

There are too many different makes and models of wireless routers to include the directions here. The first place to go is the find the owner's manual online for your make and model of router and follow the directions for setting up a time of day restriction policy. If you are having problems, call the manufacturer customer support line and have them walk you through it. You can also ask a technical friend or use one of those services like Geek Squad and have them do it for you.

After the time of day restrictions policies are in place and your router is properly configured, verify it actually works. Sometimes, there is a bug in the software running the router and the access restriction could be ignored. By verifying it's actually working, you can sleep a little better knowing your child is not online in the middle of the night.

If you want to go the low-tech route and be really sure, then simply take the family laptop and the cable modem's power supply with you when you go to bed.

Cellphones:

If your child has a cellphone, or a smartphone that you have locked down, log into your account on your service provider and setup time restrictions on your child's cellphone.

AT&T offers the Smart Controls service that costs $4.99 per month, per line. This service will allow you to set time of day, and other limits, on your child's handset.

<u>AT&T:</u> Smart Limits For Wireless

<u>Verizon:</u> Family Usage Controls

T-Mobile: http://family.t-mobile.com/

Sprint: Parental Controls

The kids will hate this, but that just confirms that it's a good thing. If they were not trying to use their cellphones in the middle of the night they would not have any reason to complain. Also, this will provide your children with an excuse with their friends. "My @!$#@-ing parents won't let me use the phone after 10!" will allow your kids to save face socially while providing you assurance that they are not using their phones at night.

After you set up the time restrictions, go online and see if there are any incoming calls or texts during the off hours. If you see any activity find out who the calls/texts are coming from and feel free to call those numbers and request they not contact your child during the night. Do this from your child's cellphone and be alert for the voice of an adult. If an adult is contacting your child from their cellphone, go to the police and report it.

If you want to go the low-tech route and be absolutely sure, then have a phone bucket and have your children surrender their cellphones to you before going to bed. Since you're paying for these devices, you are entitled to do whatever you want with them. Go for it!

If you want to know where your kids are during the day, you can enable the cell phone tracking feature. AT&T offers the Family Map service and Verizon offers the Family Locator service. By using these services, you can view where your child's handset is on a map at any time.

Family Phone Voice Mail:

If you have your young child record the outgoing message on your family voice mail system, it will let anyone who calls that number know there is a young child in the house. The public records search can be queried using your home phone number and now someone has the home phone number and street address of your child. Not a very happy thought – so, apply the voice mail security principals you learned earlier to your home voice mail.

Identification:

Make sure the social security cards, and passports, of your children are always physically secured and that you have electronic copies of these documents.

Locking up their social security cards will help prevent identity theft and securing their passports will help prevent your child from being removed from the country. If you find your child's passport is missing, immediately go to:

travel.state.gov

..and report it lost. If your child is removed from the United States it will be much more difficult to ensure their safe return.

Raising children in this age of pervasive information is very difficult. By educating your children, monitoring and limiting their activities and having a preparedness plan can help provide you with some small measure of peace of mind.

Privacy at School:

The laws protecting your privacy while you, or member of your family, at school are covered by the Family Educational Rights and Privacy Act (FERPA)

Under this act, "schools may disclose, without consent, "directory" information such as a student's name, address, telephone number, date and place of birth, honors and awards, and dates of attendance.

However, schools must tell parents and eligible students about directory information and allow parents and eligible students a reasonable amount of time to request that the school not disclose directory information about them. Schools must notify parents and eligible students annually of their rights under FERPA. The actual means of notification (special letter, inclusion in a PTA bulletin, student handbook, or newspaper article) is left to the discretion of each school."

Source: http://www2.ed.gov/policy/gen/guid/fpco/ferpa/index.html

If you are a young women who has had a privacy problem, you might think you would be safe when you went away to an undisclosed school out-of-state. The reality is, if you did not make a request to not have your information published, then anyone on the Internet will be able to find you, your school contact information and your department anonymously.

If you were studying Engineering, then anyone who would like to pay you a visit on campus would only have to locate your name, and your department. Then, access the university's class schedule and they now have enough information to conduct a hard target search for you by visiting each classroom. In a large public university with a large campus population, this information will narrow down the on campus search from, 1 in 25,000 students, down to 5-10 physical classrooms. If you are not comfortable with the availability of this information, then contact your education institution and request that they not publish your directory information.

Your school will likely provide you with an email account. This account needs to be protected because it will contain two pieces of identifiable information. Your name and your location. Try to be careful when sending emails from this account to people you do not know or when getting free furniture on Craigslist. If you meet someone and want send them an email, consider using your dirty email address that will not contain your name or your school. Your school email address can be used to search for you using the schools directory, and then use your full name to perform a public records search and find out where you live. Try to restrict your school email address to school-related activities.

Privacy in the Workplace:

After you receive your education you will then enter the workforce. Hopefully you have cyberstalked yourself and scrubbed any damaging information about yourself from social media sites and any arrest reports that could prevent you from landing your dream job. Be aware that the privacy protections afforded by law when you were a child no longer apply to the real world of business. In the business world, employers can and will monitor you and your equipment, so be very aware of how you can protect your privacy on the job.

Company Equipment:

Privacy in the workplace is a very tricky so the best policy is to assume everything you say on the company phone and do on the company computer is being monitored.

If you received a company laptop, think seriously about the risks before you do anything that is non-business related on it. No personal emails. No web browsing, unless it is related to business. Nothing.

Checking the directions to your hotel on Google maps is OK. Shopping at Victoria's Secret and reading your email on Match.com may not be.

If you want to use your company equipment for personal use, ask permission first and be sure you get a response in writing. When you get the email reply, print out a copy of the entire email, including the header information, and bring it home. You might need it later should your manager throw you under the bus. If you do not get permission, it is best not to use company equipment for any personal use.

If your company decides it needs to reduce head count, they can, and will, use any excuse to avoid having to pay unemployment benefits. All they would have to do is to request that the IT staff perform an "audit" on your laptop and smartphone, and look for any "non-business" related activity. POOF! Now they have their excuse to fire you for misusing company equipment.

Because you were fired for cause, your former employer can deny you your unemployment benefits. This happens everyday so be very careful how you use a company computer and other mobile devices. For your personal activities, buy your own laptop or tablet. Windows XP/7 based laptops are available for only a few hundred bucks and it will be money well spent.

On your corporate equipment, do not share your password or other credentials with anyone. Office politics are a fact of life and if you divulge your credentials to anyone, then the office jerk can access your systems and impersonate you while doing things that can damage your reputation or even get you fired.

If you think someone has compromised your password, or has accessed your system then change it promptly and report the incident to the IT staff. That way you have a record in case there is a problem in the future.

When traveling on business and you don't want to lug several devices around, you can use a "liveCD". A liveCD is a complete "computer on a disk". You download the CD image and burn it onto a CDROM disk using your computer. Then, put the CD into your company's laptop and reboot.

The liveCD will run on your company laptop, but there will not be any traces of your on-line activities on your corporate equipment. The Ubuntu LiveCD is an excellent choice and can be found on **www.ubuntu.com**. *Note: Any non-business related use of company equipment is risky.*

Always be aware that you have no expectation of privacy on any company equipment. If you work for the government, all of your activities on your computer, including your e-mails and browser history, are considered a public record and can be accessed. In 2009, a Lee County Sheriff's Office deputy lost his job when it was discovered he had been accessing porn sites on his office equipment.

Employee Directory:

Many companies will offer an online employee directory where your contact information can be disclosed. You can verify this by going to your employer's website and search for yourself. If the search generates your contact information, you can decide how comfortable you are with this information be made available by your employer.

If you are uncomfortable with this, you can go to your human resources department and ask that your information be blocked from online searches. Another way employers can disclose your business contact information is when calling the main phone number. Some companies will disclose your name, department, and telephone number to anyone who calls. If you are uncomfortable with this policy, then you can contact your Human Resources department and ask that this information not to be disclosed. Be aware - this is a tricky issue because you might not want to be on the radar in the HR department.

Professional Licensing:

If you are a Physician, a Nurse, Contractor, or any other state licensed professional, your licensing/certification information is considered public information and it will be disclosed to anonymous people searching for you on the Internet. Licensing information will consist of your name, town and the year you were first licensed.

Seems harmless, but it's a good starting point to begin obtaining more information about you from public records search engines. If you meet someone at a church social and you start talking and introduce yourself by your first name, "Mary", and you talk about work and say you are a nurse in the mental health field and love your job because you get to meet the most interesting people.

With a first name and a licensed profession, your new friend can go the state licensing board and within seconds know your full name, your town, and your proximate age and where you went to school. Then, thanks to public records, get your street address, age, financial information, if you voted, purchased a home, the names of your children.

By starting with only your first name and your profession, this new friend can now call you on the phone number you did not disclose and show up on your doorstep uninvited. As a licensed professional, try not to disclose your profession to anyone you don't know well.

So, if you are a.... (wait for it) ....

Acoustical Engineer, Aeronautical Engineer, Aerospace Engineer, Aesthetic Shop, Aesthetician Instructor, Aesthetician School, Agricultural Engineer, Apprentice Barber, Apprentice Gasfitter, Apprentice Plumber, Architect, Architectural Engineer, Architectural Marine Engineer, Associate Home Inspector, Astronautical Engineer, Athletic Trainer, Attorney RE Broker, Audiologist Assistant, Audiologist, Barber Instructor, Barber School, Barber Shop, Booth Renter, Booth Shop, RE Broker, Business Corporation, Ceramic Engineer, Certified Funeral Director, Certified General, Certified

Massage Therapist, Certified Public Accountant, Certified Residential, Chemical Engineer,Chiropractic Facility, Chiropractor, Civil Engineer, Construction Engineer, Control Systems Engineer, Corporation, Corrosion Engineer,Cosmetology Salon, Cosmetology School, CPA Corporation, CPA Limited Liability Company, CPA Limited Liability Partnership, CPA Partnership, Dietitian/Nutritionist, Dispensing Optician, DPA Certified Optometrist, Dual Certification, Education Waived Broker, Education Waived Salesperson, Educational Psychologist, Electrical Engineer, Electronic Engineer, Engineer In Training, Engineering Physics Engineers,Environmental Engineer, Fire Protection Engineer, Funeral Establishment, Gasfitting Corporation, Gasfitting Partnership, General Partnership, Geodetic Engineer, Geological Engineer, Geotechnical Engineer, Grade Operator In Training, Health Officers, Hearing Instrument Specialist, Heating and Ventilation Engineer, Highway Engineer, Home Inspector, Industrial Engineer, Instrumentation Engineer, Journeyman Electrician, Journeyman Gasfitter, Journeyman Gasfitter/Inspector, Journeyman Plumber, Journeyman Plumber/Inspector, Land Surveyor, Landscape Architects,Licensed Certified Social Worker, Licensed Funeral Director, Licensed Grade Full Operator, Licensed Independent Clinical Social Worker, Licensed Psychologist HSP, Licensed Psychologist NP, Licensed Psychologist, Licensed Social Worker Associate, Licensed Social Worker, Limited Liability Company, Limited Liability Partnership, Limited Partnership, Limited Practitioner, Limited Undiluted Liquefied Petroleum, Manicuring Shop, Manufacturing Engineer, Marine Engineer, Marriage and Family Therapist, Master Barber, Master Electrician, Master Gasfitter, Master Gasfitter Inspector, Master Plumber, Master Plumber/Inspector, Materials Engineer, Mechanical Engineer, Mental Health Counselor,

Metallurgical Engineer, Mining and Mineral Engineer, Naval Architecture, Nuclear Engineer, Occupational Therapist Assistant, Occupational Therapist, Optometrists, Partnership, Partnership and Corporation, Petroleum Engineer, Physical Therapist Assistant, Physical Therapist, Physical Therapy Facility, Plastics Engineer, Plumbing Corporation, Plumbing Engineer, Plumbing Partnership, Podiatrists, Public Accountants, Quality Engineer, Railroad Engineer, Real Estate Appraisal Program CE, Real Estate Appraisal School/Primary, Real Estate Program, Reciprocal Broker, Reciprocal Salesperson, Registered Aesthetician, Registered Cosmetologist, Registered Demonstrator, Registered Electrologist, Registered Electrologist Lecturer, Registered Electrology Instructor, Registered Electrology School, Registered Embalmer and Licensed Funeral Director, Registered Embalmer Apprentice, Registered Embalmer, Registered Instructor, Registered Manicuring School, Registered Manicurist, Registered Master Technician, Registered Operator, Registered Technician, Registered Unlicensed Funeral Director, Rehabilitation Therapist, Roofer, Safety Engineer, Salesperson, Sanitarians, Sanitary Engineer, Speech Pathologist Assistant, Speech Pathologist, State Licensed, Structural Engineer, Surveyor In Training, Systems Contractor, Systems Engineer, Systems Technician, Textile Engineer, TPA Certified Optometrist, Traffic Engineer, Trainee, Transitional Licensed, Transportation Engineer, Veterinarian, DHPL, Dentistry, Nursing, Nursing Home Administrator, Perfusionists, Pharmacy, Physician Assistants, Respiratory Care, Dental Hygienist, Dentist, Drug Store, Licensed Practical Nurses, Nurse Anesthetist, Nurse Midwife, Nurse Practitioner, Nursing Home Administrator, Pharmacists, Pharmacy Technician, Psychiatric Clinician, Registered Nurse....

… you are affected.

The ability to check the licensing credentials is a valuable public service. However, this licensing information can then be used to construct queries in public record search engines and those results will reveal your full identity. This clearly needs to change.

Workplace Romance:

Many people start romantic relationships at work. The HR department will often discourage workplace romances because of the fallout resulting from a faltering relationship and the increased exposure to Sexual Harassment lawsuits.

If you are considering a workplace romance, do absolutely nothing from your company equipment. No emails or texts from company property. You have no expectation of privacy on company equipment and so the intimate details of your relationship can be retrieved and sent to Human Resources. You will likely not want to have to explain the contents of the company cellphone or computer to a room full of people you don't know. Be discrete and do all of your intimate communications from the relative safety of devices you own and control.

Medical Privacy:

Your medical records are protected by The Health Insurance Portability and Accountability Act of 1996 (HIPAA); this law has sharp, pointy teeth. People have been arrested and jailed for violating this act. Personally, I would like to see a HIPAA-like act be enacted to protect all of our personal information.

In 2009, Huping Zhou was the first person in the nation to receive jail time for a HIPAA violation. Zhou had accessed confidential records without permission and went to jail for 4 months for poking around someone's medical records.

If you feel your medical related privacy has been violated, report it immediately. Document the reasons for this belief and bring it to the attention of U.S. Department of Health and Human Services at:

www.hhs.gov.

If you are concerned about your medical privacy in the real world you can take a few simple precautions to prevent the accidental disclosure of your personal ailments.

Step 1:

Use that cross-cut shredder that you purchased for the **Identity Theft** exercise and shred any medical documents before throwing them away.

This includes medical reports, laboratory results, and prescriptions. If someone sees a prescription for "Valtrex", they will know you are suffering from a viral infection.

Before throwing away your empty prescription bottles, be sure remove your personal information by destroying the label. Peel the label off of the bottle, roll it into a little ball and flush it down the toilet.

Step 2:

Keep your prescription medication in a secure bag. If you are carrying your prescription medication in your handbag or briefcase, do not take your prescription out of the bottle – instead place the bottle into a security bag.

Security bags provide locks and are used primarily for transporting and securing cash and valuable documents and are available on-line for $15-$30 depending on the size. Rifkin Security Sac offers a small bag with a lock and key.

If you take your prescription medication out of the original container, you could be looking at a jail time if you got pulled over. If you are concerned with your medical privacy, secure all prescription medication with a locking security bag. It will also provide an additional benefit in that this could save your child's life by keeping them locked away from your prescription medication.

Many kids will go through their parents medicine cabinet and use the Internet to find out if the drugs they find will get them high. If you lock away your prescription medications, this will no longer be a concern – at your house.

Vacation Privacy:

I absolutely love traveling to foreign countries. It is a great way to meet new people and get a better perspective of how people around the world live their lives. As fun as it is, travel is not without its risks so take a few precautions and you can relax and better enjoy your trip abroad.

Before your trip do a little research on the culture of the country you are visiting and pack accordingly. Leave the "USA #1" t-shirts at home as you will want to try to blend in as much as possible. Always be aware that you are on their turf and try to act accordingly.

Once you are identified as an American, you will eventually get an earful. It's happened to me, so be prepared. A simple "I didn't vote for him" will put an end to most politically charged discussions.

You might be tempted to share your upcoming travel plans on social media sites. If no one is house-sitting for you while you are away, you might want to reconsider publicly disclosing this information so you don't return from your trip to an empty house.

When posting anything online while traveling, make sure your location is not revealed. If people know you are sitting at a cafe in Brugges, they will also know you will not be home any time soon.

Take along at least 2 credit cards but only use one during your trip. If you need to use an ATM and you cannot find your bank, then look for another large bank. Never use your debit card to purchase anything and avoid using a privately owned ATM unless it is an absolute emergency.

Consider obtaining a traveler's wallet and use this to carry your cash and a copy of your documents. It will be worn under your clothes and can help protect you from pickpockets. Pickpockets are rampant in the touristy areas. My girls and I were in Paris when a group of young kids used the old "bloody nose" trick. While everyone on the metro was distracted watching this crying girl holding her nose, her accomplices went about picking the pockets of those who were listening to her sad tale of how she was mugged. After the tourists were picked clean, these kids laughed as they jumped off the train. Try to carry the minimum amount of cash and your dirty credit card in your front pocket so if you are targeted, it will only be a mild annoyance and not spoil your entire trip.

Before departing on your trip, take photographs of the front and back of your credit cards and passports. Encrypt the electronic images and save them on your camera's SDcard, a USB flash drive, and be sure to and email the encrypted copy to an email address that can be accessed through the Internet. This is your plan B. If you lose everything you will have a way to access your information and get home.

A friend of mine was in Prague a few years ago and was enjoying a refreshment in a beer garden. A woman he described as striking walked up to him and asked to join him. She wanted a chance to talk with an American and practice her English skills.

He woke up in his hotel room some time later with only his underwear and his socks. Everything else had been stolen. Whatever they put in his beer wiped his memory clean and he stumbled into the American Embassy mumbling his sister's name.

He was only able to get home quickly with the help of his sister who worked for the federal government at the time. I saw him a few weeks after it happened and his memory was still foggy. If he did not have his sister's help, then he would have had a much harder time proving his identity and obtained a replacement passport. If you have an encrypted copy of your passport, you will be able to access it from anywhere and expedite the process of getting a replacement. This type of stuff does happen, so be very mindful of your personal security while traveling and always have copies of your important documents.

Consider getting a pay-per-use cellphone when traveling. That smart phone in your hand can fetch up to $1500 US on the black market so be very aware of the profit motive in stealing your cellphone. If you are traveling in some countries, that $1500 can be several months worth of living expenses so never leave it unsecured - even for a second.

When you return home, be alert for any unusual charges on your credit card. After one of my trips, I noticed a couple of funny little charges on my credit card. I had made sure I only used one card and was able to narrow down the source of the breach. The unauthorized charges were the result of a group of people making anonymous phone calls between a hotel room in the Latin Quarter to a pay-phone in a public park near Notre Dame.

Criminals will use stolen charge cards to hide their identity while operating their businesses. My card had been compromised by the hotel's phone system when I called home.

OMG! I've Been Hacked – Now What?

If you think you have been hacked and someone has accessed or published your personal information - there are a few things you can do.

If you are a Celebrity, or a Public Official, the first thing to do is to get a lawyer and drop the mess in their lap as soon as possible. Your lawyer will be able to file "take down" notices and have your information removed from the public search engines, and their cache's. Do this immediately, as every second you delay, the greater the number of systems and search engines will contain your personal data.

If you are like the rest of us, you will have to brown-bag it and here's how:

Verify that your computer system has not been compromised by repeating the steps outlined in the "**Securing Your Computer**" exercise. If the security scan finds that there has been a security breach of your computer, then take an inventory of your sensitive data and the online activities that you have performed on that system. Every online service you have accessed with that computer has to be considered to have also been compromised.

After the security software cleans up your system, access each of your online services and look for any unusual activities on your account and change your password. If the online service contains financial related information, then follow the instructions outlined in the Identity Theft section of the **www.ftc.gov/idtheft** website and monitor your financial accounts for unusual activity.

If your financial information was compromised, then consider filing an incident report with law enforcement and your service provider. The police may or may not get involved, depending on the circumstances, but filing a report with the police will help in the event there is a problem in the future and you will now have proof that you have reported the hack.

Filing an incident report will also help law enforcement collect statistics of electronic crime for state and federal crime reporting.

Act as if you had experienced a bad breakup and follow the steps outlined earlier in the "**We've Lost Cabin Pressure**" section. This will provide you a way of removing any of the information from your system or account that may have been posted online.

If the security scan on your computer comes up empty, that could be good news and mean only one of your services may have been compromised. It is important to be able to tell the difference between a compromised email address and a compromised online account.

If your email address has been compromised, then the scammer will likely send a bunch of emails to people you may or may not know. You can tell this has happened when you start receiving rejected emails, or responses from your friends suggesting you are sending SPAM or that your account has been hacked. This is not a huge concern as the attack is probably limited to your email address. To be safe, log into your email service provider and change your password.

If someone starts impersonating you on Facebook or another online service, log into the service provider and report the incident and be sure to remember change your password.

Tell your friends and family about your experience and share how you were able to recover from the hack in case it ever happens to any of them.

Getting hacked is never fun, but it is also not the end of the world. By following the steps outlined above, you can recover from the effects of a hack attack and learn enough to better protect yourself in the future.

The Future:

The future is going to be a whole lot creepier if we do not start taking back control of our privacy today. We are no longer living in the Information Age. We are currently living in the Pervasive Information Age – where information about everything, anything, and anyone, is right at our fingertips. It is a wonderful time, but as a species were are still digesting the effects of the Information Age and do not completely understand the impact of having so much of our personal information available to anonymous disclosure.

In the future, you will also have to worry about the privacy and security of your image. There will be a service at some point where anyone can upload an image, or video clip, and this service will return your full identity. This service could have a back-end processor that scours the public information databases and report your name, where you live and who your children are and any other online identities found on social networking sites. All it would take is someone snapping a picture of you without your knowledge when you are out in public.

Smartphones in the future will contain new features that do not exist today and their existing features will become even more powerful. Broadcom, a semiconductor company, has just announced a chip for smart phones that provides ultra-precise location information - indoors and out.

The accuracy of the Broadcom 4752 chip will be able to report your position to within centimeters in a crowded mall while you do your holiday shopping. The old GPS system will report that you are at the mall, inside Target. This new chip will report that you are on the 2nd floor, buying toothpaste and you are currently reaching for a tube of "Crest Extra Whitening".

This is why Apple and Google can become trillion dollar companies as they control the platform that you use to communicate your activities both on and off line. You could start seeing ads in your online activities derived from the photos you took with your smartphone, the texts that you have sent, or your location information. I will know this has begun when I start seeing ads for heartburn medication after these companies see how much time I spend in Mexican restaurants.

Future smartphones may contain solid state chemical detectors. This will be very useful for combating terrorism by have a large distributed sensor network in the field analysing samples for pathogens or other poisons released in a terrorist attack.

An alternate use for this technology would be to configure these chemical sensors to detect the presence of alcohol. If alcohol is detected, then the location based services of the smart phone can be used to check if the mobile device is in motion and on a road. If the phone is in motion and on the road, then use the new Broadcom chip to check and report if the person is sitting in the drivers seat.

This same technology can be used to analyze air samples and detect the presence of drug activity. If the user smokes pot, crystal-meth, or any other drugs, then the mobile phone could report the drug activity to the authorities and provide to-the-centimetre positioning information to law enforcement.

This drug activity can be also reported to their health, life, and automobile insurance providers and the user could then experience an unexplained jump in their insurance premiums - or simply have their coverage terminated without a reason.

Another area of privacy concern could be stealth drug and genetic testing. If an employer is self-insured, they may want to minimize their financial exposure to future health related claims and have you tested for drug and genetic predispositions to cancer without your knowledge or consent. All they would have to do is go to your workstation and get a sample of your hair and send it to a testing lab.

If the lab reports signs of drug use in the past year, assuming your hair is 6 inches long and grows at a rate of ½ inch a month, they can then subject you to a surprise formal drug test.

Should the genetic testing return that you're predisposed to cancer, then you can be put on a list and be the first to be laid off when a company needs to downsize. It is technically possible and it would be very difficult for anyone to prove that their employer had violated their medical privacy.

Your mobile device could soon become your credit card and you will be able to make purchases with a simple wave of your phone. Hackers will try to steal your phone, or your information, and clone your financial identity to commit fraud. With biometric authentication, your fingerprint will be valuable and thieves will try to make an impression they can use to withdraw funds from your bank accounts. All they would need is some silly-putty and your fingerprint.

There is a large amount of brand new technology in the pipeline and yet, we have not fully digested the effects of what we have now. The trend is toward more information and more interconnections to develop a more intimate consumer profile that can be used for advertising. So it is up to us to decide for ourselves what information we are going to disclose and we should always try to be aware of the consequences of trading our privacy for a little convenience.

Benjamin Franklin said in 1759:

"Those who would give up essential liberty to purchase a little temporary safety deserve neither liberty nor safety."

This same line of thinking can be applied to privacy.

Summary:

The privacy situation in the country is a very serious concern, but the good news is you can do something about it today to better protect yourself and your family. By following the steps we've discussed earlier you can take back control of your privacy and help reduce your chances of having a problem in your future. You are likely now more aware of the quantity and scope of your personal information sitting on machines around the world and the impact it can have on your life.

Every exercise in this book was intended to help you create a buffer between your virtual world activities and your physical world activities. This buffer is to separate your two worlds and to prevent activities that occur in the virtual world from spilling over and impacting you in your real life.

Your "dirty" credit card, cellphone, and online identities, are all used to help prevent your information from becoming compromised and linked directly to you. If there is a problem with any of these identities, you can simply discard them and obtain a new one while your real identity is protected.

The auto-stalking exercise was performed to develop your online privacy profile. Like many people, you were probably not fully aware of the amount of your personal information that is available on the Internet. Much of this information was acquired and posted without your knowledge and consent and by stalking yourself online, you can now take back control of your privacy and have those records removed.

You are in complete control over what information you post, so be very aware of any potential real world consequences of your actions. As we've seen, you can not *unpublish* what you have posted, so pause for a second before hitting that "Send" key. It can save you a lot of trouble in your future.

Before posting any information about yourself, or others, try to image a real-world scenario and see if you would still disclose that information. For example:

Action: Upload Contact list to social media site
Question: Would you hand over your address book to a stranger?

Action: Update profile with cell phone number
Question: Would you hand your cell phone number to someone you do not know?

Action: Post photos
Question: Would you post that photo on your office door?

Unlike your personal online activities, you have little control over what information is posted about you by public records search queries unless you have taken steps to protect your privacy.

The public records laws are what really need to change. They were written well before the pervasive information age and need to be updated to reflect the current environment. Public records access is the main threat to your physical security and privacy of your family.

The republishing of your information allows anyone in the world with an Internet connection to pierce that membrane separating the virtual from the physical world.

There are ways to use existing cryptographic techniques to secure public records and provide the same level of public service while maintaining the security of the information and preserving the privacy of the individuals.

The technology is here. We just need the will.

How to Help:

Share your new found privacy awareness with your friends and family. We are fighting an uphill battle and companies are making billions of dollars under the current system. If enough people get involved and take a stand, then the current system will change to our mutual benefit.

Write your lawmakers to get the public records laws changed and encourage them to enact laws that protect **all** of your personal information. Privacy is often ignored until it has been violated and by then it is too late. If we let the lawmakers know that we value our privacy and want them to help protect us, then they will have a strong incentive to take the privacy issue seriously.

Support privacy non-profits – they are the proverbial Davids going up against the Goliaths of big business. Big businesses are well funded organizations that feeds on your private information. Any attempts to restrict the source of their revenue will be met with stiff resistance.

These non-profits that are fighting for your privacy rights include:

Privacy Rights Clearinghouse:
www.privacyrights.org

World Privacy Forum:
www.worldprivacyforum.org

Electronic Frontier Foundation:
www.eff.org

Electronic Privacy Information Center
http://www.epic.org/

If enough people demand, not ask, but **demand** their privacy rights, the lawmakers will take notice and change the outdated public records laws and force businesses to protect your information to better serve and protect, you and your family.

About the Author:

I'm really not one - I'm just a guy who's concerned enough to try to do something about the privacy issue. If any of this information has raised your awareness of how important it is to protect your personal privacy, then I am grateful that this has helped you in some small way.

We have covered a lot of ground and I hope this didn't sound too much like stereo instructions. If you wish to contact me, please feel free to send an email to:

alan@smartwomansprivacy.com

It has been a pretty intense month of sitting in front of the computer, so I'm now going to shut these machines off and go for a ride on the bike path – right after I check Facebook.

Enjoy your afternoon!

Epilogue:

"pmf", the hacker from operation CyberSnare, opened up a cupcake shop on the East Coast.

Special Agent Stacy Bauerschmidt died in 2008 after a two year battle with cancer. She was one of my all-time favorite people and I miss her.

Acknowledgments:

I would like to take this time to thank the people who helped make this project possible – though many of them are now busily scrubbing their information from the Internet.

Many thanks go to my sister, Jules, and my Mom for their input and editing efforts that made it possible to go from initial concept to publication in about 7 weeks.

Thanks go out to my good friend Laura at DaisyBee Designz, for putting together the book cover and website. You can see her work at:

www.daisybeedesignz.com

Thanks go to my friend, Miles Mathis, who supplied the image for the book cover. His amazing art can be seen at:

www.milesmathis.com

I would also like to thank James Altucher, for showing me this can be done. His hilariously honest blog can be found at

www.jamesaltucher.com

Privacy Enhancement Checklist

Financial Identity:

Get your free credit report every year
look for accounts / queries you do not recognize. Report it!

Get two credit cards
Clean – Use in physical world
Dirty – On the Internet

Reduce Credit card limit
1.5-2X largest month in the last year

Monitor your statements for unusual activity

Consider using Gift cards online

Never use your Debit card to make purchases

Only use your ATM cards at your bank, or other large bank.

Avoid privately owned ATMs

Get and use a good document shredder

Contact your banks and “opt-out”

For online payment systems, like Paypal, use a small separate bank account

Cellphone/Smartphone:

Always assume you will lose your cellphone

Minimize personal information on your device

Use a strong screen password
Never disclose your password
Don't enter your password in front of someone you do not trust

Block CallerID when calling numbers you do not know.

Disable unnecessary geo-location (GPS) functions
Maps – Yes
Photo – No
Social Media Clients – No.
Ask yourself if location access is necessary

Be wary of mobile apps that want access to your personal information and networking services

Turn off Wi-Fi/Bluetooth when not in use

Log off your apps when not in use
Facebook / LinkedIn / Social Media
Banking/Credit Card/ Financial Apps

Minimize use of geo-locating services

Configure mobile web browser for privacy-mode

Minimize information in your contact list

Minimize personal information in mobile email configuration

Disable iCloud / Cloud data services for personally sensitive information.

Frequently purge text messages

Delete emails that is not required to save

Password protect your cellphone backup on your computer

Use different password

Never leave your cellphone unattended!

Open Purse

Crammed in back pocket

On table or the bar

In car

Voice mail - Do not reveal any identifiable information.

Wipe your mobile device before discarding

If stolen immediately notify your carrier and attempt to have them remotely “wipe” your device and lock it out of the network.

Laptop / Desktop / Tablet:

Assume your laptop will be stolen!

Don't use a personal information as your account name

Use a strong password

Set your internet browser to privacy mode
- Delete history
- Delete Cookies on close
- Select "Do Not Track"
- Chrome: Select maximum privacy mode
- Set to never remember passwords / account information

Install Anti-virus / Anti Malware software
- Scan / Update frequently!

Be VERY careful clicking on links in email / on Facebook or other social networking sites
- If button states asks to give permission: Click Cancel and block application

Do use unknown Flash-drives / SDcard in your system. Scan with AV software FIRST!

If any email contains an attachment – scan with AV software before opening. Without exception

When forwarding an email, strip out the email Information of others before sending

When sending email to a group, use the BCC function

Do not lend your laptop to anyone you do not trust A LOT!

Do not let anyone have physical access to your desktop machine – if you do then perform a security scan to ensure the system has not been tampered with

Home Networking:

Consider not broadcasting your SSID of your wireless router

Set your SSID to something innocuous – Do not use your street address / phone number / pet name or anything identifiable

Append "_nomap" to your SSID to prevent Google and other companies from tracking the physical location of your wireless router.

Do use a strong password, different than the SSID, to access your Wi-Fi network.

Use WPA2 and a strong password to block unauthorized access

Consider MAC filtering to restrict access to known devices

Refresh your IP address

Before You Go Online:

Create several identities
- Personal or "Clean"
- Shopping or "Grey"
- Throwaway or "Dirty"

Always use a strong password
Never share with anyone
Never share with any other service

Practice Safe Computing:

Update all of your software

Be wary of emails contains links or attachments.

Always scan any attachment or download

Beware of unknown removable media.
Always scan first

SSL everywhere. Always use "https//" on any website you need to log in to

Backup you systems frequently and secure with a strong password

When disposing of your computer,be sure to completely scrub the hard drive securely

Online Privacy Profile:

Frequently stalk yourself on the Internet

Verify privacy settings of social media search results

Remove public records search entries by "opting-out"

Consider getting a PO Box and updating your Public Records / Country Clerk's office

Remove any offending links from search engines.
Remember include the cached copy

Get criminal activity sealed or expunged.
Remove all online references

Facebook/Social Media:

Always assume your account will be hacked

Minimize the amount of personal information you post:

No phone numbers
No Physical Address
No REAL email addresses
No Birth dates
Hide Friends

Limit access to ONLY people you know

Accept friend request only from people you know in the real world

Turn off all application platform:

No games / jokes / funny pages
They could steal your personal information

Require that you get to review anything anyone posts to your Wall/Page before being published

Any link/button/etc that asks permission to access your information. Press cancel / and delete

Any link/button that asks for your password – even if it appears to be from a known site - close window. Do not lose your login credentials.

Do not post compromising photos of yourself
They will haunt you forever

Do not post photos anything that could identify you in the real world:

Examples: License plate. Driver License, Landmarks, Password

Frequently purge your profile and messages: Only keep a few months of activity up at any time.

Turn off linked accounts

Enable secure connection / SSL

Opt-out of 3rd party ads

Hide family and friends lists

No groups:
Personal stuff on Facebook.
Business stuff on LinkedIn

Do not post anything on Facebook or any other social media site that you would not feel comfortable wearing on a t-shirt at the police station or nursing home.

Home Phone (do people still have those?):

Get an unlisted phone number

Use Google voice

On your voice-mail or answering machine – Do not reveal any identifiable information like your name or address.

Use a strong voice-mail password and employ good password security.

Relationships and Dating:

No identifiable information in your user-name
No names / Dates / Year

Fuzz your required personal information that could identify you in real life
Age / Town / Children / Profession

If using a photo – make sure image is not geotagged or contain personal information.

Don't post photos of your children or anyone else without asking their permission first

Use your "Dirty" email address.

Do not use your work computer to email.
They will be able to know where you are employed before you disclose that information.

Get a pay per use cellphone used exclusively for dating.

Never text from your Clean phone to numbers you do not know

Never give out your work,home and real cellphone number until you are comfortable doing so.

Do try to get as much information about your new friend, while being careful about what you disclose about yourself.

Bad Breakup:

Change all of your passwords

Do not post anything that may upset your ex
- Derogatory comments
- Photos of you and your new friend

Do not accept new friend requests on social media sites

Report any harassment or threatening behavior

Be aware of electronic tracking

Stalking/ Harassment:

Preserve all communications

If you feel you are unsafe - inform the police

Unmask blocked calls, or dump blocked call to voice mail

Protecting your Children:

Search for your children online

Have a current photograph of your children

Be alert to anyone talking pictures of your children

Establish a secret code word

Block all communication activity at night

Call anyone you find communicating with your child after hours on your child's cell phone

Install a key logger in your child's computer and block them from using any other communication device in your home

No children on outgoing voice mail message

Secure their SSN, identification and passports and have digital copies available.
If they are missing report it.

Privacy at School:

Ask to be removed from the schools public directory

Reconsider allowing the school to use your child's image or name

Protect your school email address.

Privacy at Work:

Assume everything you do on company equipment is monitored

No personal use of company equipment unless you first obtain written permission

If concerned, ask to be removed from the company directory

If professionally licensed, use a PO box in another town

Be very careful with personal relationships at work

Medical Privacy:

If you feel your medical privacy has been violated, report it

Secure all prescription medication in a locking bag

Securely destroy all medical related information:
- Lab reports
- Prescription and their labels

Vacation Privacy:

Don't post travel plans on social media sites

Try to blend in and avoid political discussions

Take photos of your ID and credit cards and carry secured copies

Only use one credit card. Never use your debit card to make purchases

Only use Bank ATM's - preferably yours
Be aware of your personal security at all times

Be alert of unusual activities on your credit cards

Automobile:

No vanity plates
No distinguishing stickers or other adornments
Never leave purse, laptop or cellphone unattended.

Appendix I – IV

Appendix I Smartphone Privacy

iPhone:

Turn Wi-Fi ON/OFF

Tap "Settings"
Toggle "Wi-Fi : ON/OFF
Toggle "Ask to join" ON

Location Services

Tap	"Settings"
Tap	Location Services
Toggle	ON/OFF (your choice)
Camera	OFF
Compass	ON
Maps	OFF
Safari	OFF

Consider turning off for any app that does not have a legitimate need for your location

Bluetooth:

Tap "Settings"
Tap "General"
Bluetooth

Toggle : OFF till needed

Turn Screen lock ON:

Tap "Settings"
Tap "General"
Auto-Lock: 2 minutes
Pass code Lock: ON

Enter a pass code: Avoid using your ATM PIN, birthday, last 4 of your SSN or phone number.

Mail Contact, Calendar

Tap "Settings"
Tap "Mail Contact, Calendar"

Go through each account and remove personal information

Privacy Mode Browsing

Tap "Settings"
Tap "Safari"
Toggle "Private Browsing" ON
Accept Cookies: from visited

Tap Clear History
Tap Clear Cookies and Data

Fraud Warning: ON
Block Pop-ups: ON

Android:

Turn Wi-Fi ON/OFF

Tap “Settings” then Wi-Fi OFF/ON

Location Services

Tap “Settings” then Location Services

Google's Location Services :ON/OFF
GPS satellites: ON/OFF
Location and Google Search : ON/OFF

Consider turning these off until you need them to help prevent tracking your mobile device

Bluetooth:

Tap “Settings” Bluetooth OFF/ON

Consider turning these off until you need them to help prevent tracking your mobile device

Turn Screen lock ON:

Screen Lock: ON

Select type you want

Mail Contact, Calendar

Go through each account and scrub any personal information. Clean account, can just have your first name. Dirty accounts make up some initials.

Privacy Mode Browsing

Tap: Browser
Tap: Options button
Tap: Privacy and Security
Tap: clear cache
Tap: Clear History
Tap: Clear Cookies
Tap: Accept Cookies (no cookies)
Tap: Remember Form Data - OFF
Tap: Clear Form Data
Tap: Enable Location - OFF
Tap: Clear location Access
Tap: Remember passwords – OFF
Tap: Clear Passwords

Appendix II Browser Privacy

FireFox:

Click on: FireFox → Option->Options

Click on: Privacy Tab

Toggle: Tracking ON
Tell websites I do not want to be tracked

History: Set to "Never remember History"

Click on: Security Tab
Warn me when site install add-ons: ON
Block reported attack sites: ON
Block reported web forgeries: ON
Remember passwords: OFF

Chrome:

Click "Wrench" (upper right corner)
Click "New Incognito" window
Note: It's only for that session.
When you restart chrome you will have to toggle "incognito mode" with <ctrl><shift><n>

Consider switching to Firefox/Explorer where you do not have to toggle the privacy mode every time you use the browser

Explorer:

Delete everything from browser
Press: <ctrl> <shift> <p>
Click on “Gear” (upper right corner)
Click “Internet Options”
Click “Privacy” tab
Set slider to “High”
Toggle “Never allow websites to request your physical location-based: ON

Safari:

Click Safari → Private Browsing, and then click OK

Note: It's only for that session. When you restart safari you will have to do this again

Consider switching to Firefox where you do not have to toggle the privacy mode every time you use the browser

Appendix III Email Clients

Thunderbird:

Compose Email in plain text:

Click on : Tools -> Account Settings -> Composition & Addressing -> Compose messages in HTML format for each account.

View Email in Text Format:

Click: View->Message Body As → Plain Text

Remove personal Information:

Click on : Tools -> Account Settings

For each account look at the "Your Name" setting and change accordingly

Return Receipts:

Click on Tools->Options->Advanced->Return Receipts

Make sure setting is "Ask me" or "Never Send"

MS Outlook:

On the Tools menu, click Trust Center, and then click Privacy Options.

Then click E-mail Security category.

Make sure **Read all standard mail in plain text** and **Read all digitally singed mail in plain text** are checked as Read as Plain Text.
Click OK.

MacMail:

Make sure Mac OS X Mail is not running.

Launch Terminal.

Type "defaults write com.apple.mail PreferPlainText -bool TRUE'"

Do not include the quotation marks.

Then press *Enter.*

Appendix IV Encryption

Windows XP Professional:

How to Encrypt a Folder

Click **Start**, point to **All Programs**, point to **Accessories**, and then click **Windows Explorer**.

Locate and right-click the folder that you want to encrypt, and then click **Properties**.

On the **General** tab, click **Advanced**.

Under **Compress or Encrypt attributes**, select the **Encrypt contents to secure data** check box, and then click **OK**.

Click **OK**.

In the **Confirm Attribute Changes** dialog box that appears, use one of the following steps:

If you want to encrypt only the folder, click **Apply changes to this folder only**, and then click **OK**.

If you want to encrypt the existing folder contents along with the folder, click **Apply changes to this folder, subfolders and files**, and then click **OK**.

Windows 7 - Professional:

To Encrypt a Folder or File

Right-click the folder or file you want to encrypt, and then click Properties.

Click the General tab, and then click Advanced.

Select the Encrypt contents to secure data check box, and then click OK.

To Decrypt a Folder or File

Right-click the folder or file you want to decrypt, and then click **Properties**.

Click the **General** tab, and then click **Advanced**.

Clear the "**Encrypt contents to secure data**" check box, and then click OK.

Windows 7 – All Versions:

7-Zip:

The easiest way encrypt your sensitive files is use the archive package "7-zip" than can be downloaded from: **www.7-zip.org**.

Encrypting Files/Folders:

Once installed, right-click on any files or folders that you want to encrypt and select **7-Zip->Add to Archive**. There you will be prompted to enter a password.

Enter your password and press "OK". Now you can delete the original files.

Decrypting Files/Folders:

Right-click on the encrypted file and select

7-Zip->Open Archive.

Drag the archive to you Desktop and enter your password at the prompt.

GNU Privacy Guard

For all versions of Windows, download and install GNU Privacy Guard from : **www.gnupg.org**.

Once installed, open the program "Kleopatra" and then enter <CTRL-N> to create a new OpenPGP keypair.

Fill out the information any way you want and use one of your email addresses you have previously set up.

When prompted, enter a passphrase to use to manage your new key.

You've just created a key so make a backup of your keypair and save it on another system. If you lose this keypair, you will not be able to access your encrypted files.

To Encrypt a file or folder:

Right-click on the file/folder and select "sign and encrypt" and click "Next".

You will now see a window with your key,
Select your new key and click "Add" then click "Encrypt". Now you can delete the unencrypted version

To Decrypt an encrypted file or folder:

Right-click on the file/folder and select "Decrypt and Verify" and click "Next".

Enter your key passphrase and click "Decrypt/Verify"

TrueCrypt:

TrueCrypt is a free application that lets you create encrypted virtual disks and can be downloaded from: **www.truecrypt.org**. It is especially useful for encrypting the contents of portable media such as USB flash drives.

After installing the package, you can create an encrypted volume that you can use to protect your sensitive files.

Run **TrueCrypt** and click on **Create Volume** then **Next**, and **Next**. At the **Volume Location** prompt, enter the name you want to use for your encrypted folder. Ex: testfolder

Then click **Next** and enter the size of the folder you want. It doesn't matter if it is too small as you can always create a larger volume and copy your files over. Click **Next** and enter the **Volume Password** to use – **remember it**! Click **Next** and then **Format.** Now you have an encrypted folder to store your files. To mount your new folder, click on **Select File,** then locate your encrypted file "testfolder" and then click **Mount.** Enter you password at the prompt and now you can start filling the volume with your sensitive files.

Mac OS X 10.4:

To set up FileVault on your computer:

Choose **Apple menu > System Preferences** and click **Security**.

If the Security preferences pane is locked, click the **lock icon** and type an administrator name and password.

If Security preferences shows that a master password has not been set, click **Set Master Password** and enter a password in the Master Password box.

Enter the password again in the Verify box.

Use the Hint box to help you remember the password.

Click **OK**.

Click "**Turn on FileVault**" and read the message that appears. If you want to be sure your deleted files can never be recovered, click "**Use secure erase.**"

1. Click "**Turn on FileVault**" in the dialog, or click Cancel to stop.